"*I consider Hal and Sidra Stone to be on the cutting edge of new and effective forms of transforming therapy. Their Voice Dialogue work is original and brilliant. This book embodies the application of that work to creating intimate relationships. We desperately need this book.*"

John Bradshaw
Author of *Homecoming* and *Family Secrets*

"*As a Catholic priest, I have been excited and appreciative of the Voice Dialogue method described in* Embracing Our Selves. *Now, the Drs. Stone have extended their ideas and brought to us this remarkable companion volume,* Embracing Each Other. *As in the first book, they continue to honor and facilitate the process of becoming holy, which has always been the call of our religious tradition and other traditions as well.*"

Fr. Bill Whittier
Catholic Priest
Teacher and Counselor

"*Hal and Sidra Stone have utilized careful, perceptive clinical observation to develop a clean theoretical construct which is then presented in an elegant, understandable writing style. I strongly recommend this book to professionals and non-professionals alike.*"

G. Rick Smith, M.D.
Associate Professor of Psychiatry
and Vice Chairman of Research for Medical Science
University of Arkansas

"*In* Embracing Our Selves, *the Drs. Stone described the psychology of selves and the Voice Dialogue process which is the single best tool I've found in 23 years of psychiatric practice. In* Embracing Each Other, *they extended their non-judgmental, non-pathologizing approach to the sphere of personal relationships. I cannot recommend this book strongly enough to the reading public.*"

Phil Bohnert, M.D.
Assistant Professor of Psychiatry and Family Practice
Baylor College of Medicine

Embracing Each Other

Embracing Each Other

How to Make All Your
Relationships
Work for You

Hal Stone, Ph.D. & Sidra Stone, Ph.D.

Delos, Inc.

Delos, Inc.
P. O. Box 604
Albion, CA 95410-0604
Telephone (707) 937-2424
Fax (707) 937-4119
Email delos@mcn.org
Website: http://www.delos-inc.com

Cover Design: Mary Ann Casler
Book cover photo: Sam Young
Typography: Harrington-Young, Albany, California

The authors of this book do not dispense medical advice nor prescribe the use of any technique as a form of treatment for physical or mental problems without the advice of a physician whether directly or indirectly. In the event you use any of the information in this book, neither the authors nor the publisher can assume any responsibility for your actions. The intent of the authors is only to offer information of a general nature to help you in your quest for personal growth.

First printing, September 1989

ISBN 1-56557-062-6 – $13.95
Printed in United States
10   9

To
Elizabeth, Claudia, and Recha Winkelman
and
Joshua and Judith Stone

Contents

Acknowledgments

To all the loved ones, the teachers, the colleagues, and the clients who have shared their depths with us and to everyone who has supported us on our journey, we would like to express our deepest gratitude and love for the gifts you have given us along our way. And to all the adversaries who challenged us and pushed us further than we might have gone, we would like to express our thanks for teaching us the things we did not want to learn. Without all of you, this book would never have been written.

Introduction

This is a book about relationship, relationship as an adventure, a never-ending journey into the unknown. It is about relationship as a teacher who will lead us in an exploration of both the world outside and the world within, guiding us in our own inexorable evolution of consciousness. We have based this book upon our own personal experience in relationships and upon the experiences of the many people who have shared their relationships with us.

This is not a book with easy answers for "solving problems" and making relationships "work" because we have noticed over the years that there are no easy answers. It is, instead, a book that will initiate the reader into the amazing complexities of relating to another and show the unbelievably rich gifts that relationships can bring.

Relationship, in this way of thinking, is a journey of the soul. Although this may sound a bit formidable, the journey is exciting, full of unexpected twists and turns and, surprisingly enough, a very natural one. It is all a question of trust.

Unfortunately, few of us have been raised to trust relationships and to learn from them. We have been raised,
instead, to conduct relationships "appropriately," to figure
out how to handle and generally to control our relationships
so that neither we, nor others, will be uncomfortable at any
time. Most of our concern in relationship, whether it be with
a lover, a family member, a fellow worker, or a teacher,
centers upon doing away with discomforts, solving problems, and avoiding conflict.

Our culture is primarily rational and result-oriented in
its outlook, and this is reflected in our relationships. We want
them to work flawlessly and efficiently. We read books on
how to improve them, learn techniques of analysis and
communication and conflict resolution. Still, our relationships are never as smooth and well-functioning as we imagine
they should be. Whether we are trying to discipline a child,
speak with our parents, relate to a co-worker, or reconnect
with a lover, matters can become inexplicably complicated.

Somehow, in this mechanistic way of looking at things,
most of us feel that if we just figure out the way a relationship
works, we should never again be unhappy, misunderstood,
or in any way uncomfortable. We (or our Inner Perfectionists) carry a picture in our heads of a mature, loving, well-
adjusted pair of individuals who are able to connect deeply,
be mutually supporting, and relate with great common
sense. This ideal couple can solve problems by sitting down
and sensibly talking them over, listening, respecting, and
effectively communicating with one another, but never hurting one another's feelings, never being totally confused, and
never questioning basic assumptions. There is always a clear
understanding of what form the relationship will assume and
how it will evolve.

These fantasies are supported by many of the television
sitcoms that portray idealized family constellations. Over the
years, however, we have noticed that life rarely works that
way; at least it has not seemed to work that way for the people
we have met. Things are a bit more complex, and people,

bless them, are the most complicated of all. Each of us is made up of many parts or selves. Therefore, we do not behave in a fully predictable and consistent fashion, and our relationships are inevitably complicated.

Since none of us is a single psychological entity, it is misleading to think of ourselves in this way. When we are in a relationship, it is not just two people who sit down for a nice, friendly, sensible chat. We each have within us numerous selves or subpersonalities, each one vying for attention, trying to get its needs met. The "sensible little chat" is a bit more like two large family groups trying to talk with one another. These inner families are far from homogeneous in outlook. They are bickering amongst themselves even as we try to relate in a consistent fashion to another person. The more emotional the subject matter, the more these selves that make up our inner family disagree with one another.

As the scope of our own consciousness increases, we are able to access more and more of these selves. We become more aware of what is happening, both within ourselves and within our relationships. This growth in consciousness gives to our relationships added depth and complexity, and gives each one of us a greater feeling of solidity.

The Gift of Relationship

The gift of relationship is the gift of these selves. A truly committed relationship is a journey of exploration into the very depths of one's own being. It provides us with the opportunity to look within and to meet an infinite variety of these selves that make up our inner families. Each of these selves has its own physiological characteristics, point of view, and unique ability to observe and understand the world about us. Each has its own history and contributes its own particular kind of information, energy, and ability to relate. The more selves we can access, the richer and more complete our lives and relationships will be.

Relationship, when fully lived, brings each of us face to

face with ever-increasing numbers of these selves. It forces us to take responsibility for this entire inner family, no matter how chaotic or embarrassing the "family members" may be. But it also brings to us the gifts of the selves; each, indeed, has its own gift to offer.

The Journey of Relationship

There are two distinct paths to follow in relationship. Those who follow the first remain cautious, allowing the selves that have served them so well in the past to continue to protect them. Their behavior becomes quite predictable, stereotypical, maybe even rigid. They keep to the familiar and the safe. Any parts or selves that threaten to upset the equilibrium of any of their relationships are kept in exile. Life is confined to the few familiar selves that seem to interact favorably, and quietly, with others. Those who follow this path usually identify with the more rational, problem-solving selves, carefully guarding against any selves that might cause trouble, in most cases disowning them totally. Sometimes people who follow this path narrow their lives down to a few selves that keep others at a distance, or that interact compulsively and/or destructively in relationship to other people.

We all know people who have done this; each of us has certainly done so at some time in our own life. This is a perfectly natural reaction to a relationship that we value and wish to protect. We quickly disown the selves that represent our selfishness, flirtatiousness, sensuality, adventurousness, intellect, territoriality, shyness, or whatever it is that the other person in our lives does not like. *Without even thinking, we give up special parts of ourselves, or we stop participating in certain pleasurable activities, in order to safeguard the relationship. We narrow down our lives and live within the safe perimeter of a few acceptable selves.* This, in fact, has been the pattern in the past and has worked very well for many people.

Very loving long-term relationships are possible following this model.

However, there is an extremely exciting and rewarding alternative. *This alternative is to use relationship of all kinds as a constant challenge, as a teacher, as the guide in our own personal evolution of consciousness.* Instead of trying to maintain the status quo, those who choose this path can accept each new interaction (particularly the uncomfortable ones) as a new possibility presented and can view relationship as a never-ending voyage of discovery. *There are, perhaps, an infinite number of selves within us. Each has something to teach us. Each brings added richness to our perception of the world around us. Relationship challenges more and more of these selves to emerge as we become ever more deeply involved with another human being.*

We have written this book as a guide for those who are interested in taking this particular journey of exploration. Our work is based upon the belief that relationship has within itself a spark of the divine, and that in truly trusting relationship as a teacher, each of us will eventually be brought to ourselves, to the deepest and purest essence of our humanity, which is, by nature, divine.

PART I

Meeting
Our Selves

1

The Psychology of Selves

This chapter summarizes our way of looking at the development of personality. It introduces our concept of selves and of bonding patterns in relationship and presents our particular view of the consciousness process. This is the basic theoretical framework into which the remaining chapters fit. For those readers familiar with our work, this can be used as an update as well as a review, because we have expanded our thinking about bonding patterns considerably. Most of this material, however, is given a more comprehensive treatment in our book, *Embracing Our Selves*, published by Nataraj Publishing. It is intended as a companion to this book. It not only presents a thorough picture of the different selves that inhabit our psyche, it also provides a definitive description of Voice Dialogue, the process we developed that has been the main tool used in our explorations of relationship.

The Development of the Selves

Most of us are familiar with the outer family into which we were born. We have parents and grandparents, brothers, sisters and cousins, aunts and uncles. We may also have close friends who function as family members and who, at times, are closer to us than our actual families. Learning about our families and how we fit into them is a very important part of the growing-up process.

What is fascinating to consider, and what is a new idea for most people, is that we have an inner family as well as an outer one. This inner family is influenced, first of all, by those closest to us. It consists, at first, of selves that resemble the personality patterns of our family members, friends, teachers, or anyone who has had any kind of influence over us, or, conversely, it consists of the personality characteristics (or selves) that represent the exact opposite patterns.

Learning about this inner family is a very important part of personal growth and absolutely necessary for the understanding of our relationships, since the members of this inner family, or "selves," as we like to call them, are often in control of our behavior. If we do not understand the pressures they exert, then we are really not in charge of our lives.

How does this inner family develop? As we grow in a particular family and culture, each of us is indoctrinated with certain ideas about the kind of person we should be. Since we are very vulnerable as infants and children, it is important that we be the "kind of person we should be," and we behave in a way that keeps us safe and loved and cared for. This need to protect our basic vulnerability results in the development of our personality—the development of the primary "selves" that define us to ourselves and to the world.

We each are born into this world in an extremely vulnerable condition. This initial self remains as a vulnerable child, a child of the utmost sensitivity, who carries with it the ability to relate intimately to others. This child can be seen as the doorway to our most profound states of being, to our souls, if you wish. It is this child who essentially carries our psychic fingerprint, and it is this child that we spend our lives protecting at all costs. Other selves develop within us early in life to stand between this child and other people so that nobody will ever be able to harm it. This is both natural and necessary, but by the time we are adults and are functioning well in the world, the selves that were developed earlier have a tendency to be overly protective.

These selves have usually decided that the best way to protect the vulnerable inner child is to keep it well-hidden, fully out of the reach of any other human being (though it may be acceptable for the child to interact with a pet). Unfortunately, this also keeps the vulnerable child out of relationships and deprives it of what it so dearly wishes—a deep and honest connection with other human beings. This keeps many of us from the intimacy we seek in relationship, since intimacy requires the presence of the vulnerable child. It is only with access to this child that we can truly know ourselves and others.

The first of the protective selves to develop is called the protector/controller because it protects the vulnerable child and controls both our behavior and that of the people around us. This protector/controller emerges surprisingly early in life. It looks about, notices what behavior is rewarded and what is punished, makes sense of the rules of the world it sees around it, and sets up a code of behavior for us. It is constantly looking for more information and will change its rules to accommodate it. This basically rational self explains the world, and ourselves, to us and provides us with the frame of reference within which we will view our surroundings.

When the protector/controller is in complete charge of our lives, as it so often is, no input is permitted that might upset the status quo or lead us to question cherished beliefs and characteristic ways of being. The role of this self is to protect the child and, in doing so, it usually keeps the child from real contact with others.

The protector/controller has as its major ally, the pusher. This self is ever-alert to what must be done next. The pusher makes lists, prompts us to complete tasks, keeps us busy and productive so that our vulnerable child will feel that we are good and that people will admire us. It is less than helpful, however, when we are trying to relax. It also tends to interfere with intimacy. If we are never in a relationship, the pusher can continue to run our lives; there is nobody to question its pre-eminence. We are prodigiously productive and greatly admired, but have not learned how to stand still long enough to make meaningful contact with someone.

Another major ally of the protector/controller is the perfectionist. Just as its name implies, this part of us sets goals of perfection, usually on all fronts. We must look perfect, be perfect, have the perfect relationship, work flawlessly, produce perfect children, so that nobody will ever criticize us and the vulnerable child will remain safe. The perfectionist has no tolerance for human frailty, little appreciation of reality, and can be pretty harsh in its view of relationship.

This self is greatly rewarded by our society and usually encouraged by our families, since it makes their internal perfectionists feel successful. The perfectionist has its place, of course. We certainly need it to set standards in some areas, such as performing surgery or designing earthquake-proof buildings, but it can be a tragically inappropriate taskmaster in our personal lives. A deeply committed relationship will lessen the power of the perfectionist and allow us to explore ourselves and others in a more forgiving fashion.

The inner critic works along with the perfectionist to protect the vulnerable child. If the critic catches all of our mistakes and inadequacies before anyone else does, or so the reasoning goes, there will be nothing about us to displease anyone, and our vulnerable child will be safe from criticism.

Unfortunately, by the time the average inner critic is finished with us, our self-esteem is shot to pieces and we feel totally unlovable. We must then go back to our old friends, the pusher and the perfectionist, and work even harder to make ourselves acceptable.

Another self that helps to make us acceptable is the pleaser. The pleaser is exquisitely sensitive to the needs and feelings of others and gently guides us in the delicate task of meeting those needs, so that others will think highly of us and be similarly understanding of our needs. This, too, is designed to protect the vulnerable child. Unfortunately, if we listen to the pleaser all the time, we tend to forget our own needs and to totally neglect our inner child. In a committed relationship we are required to look past the pleaser within ourselves and see what it is that is truly important to us. This often results in the greatest spurts of growth for both people concerned.

When these selves, and the many others whose job it is to protect our vulnerable child, are used in a constructive fashion, they can aid us on the journey of self-discovery. However, when they take over completely, they can prevent us from experimentation and can keep us from bringing the totality of our imperfect, complex, contradictory and exciting selves into our relationships. They may prevent us from realizing the possibilities that exist beyond the known and the familiar.

The Primary Selves:
The Development of Personality

By the time we are adults, we have an amazing family operating inside of ourselves, generally much larger than our outer family. We usually are identified with the value structure of our original protector/controller and the parts that he or she has helped bring into the world in order to protect us. These represent our *primary selves*.

There are also the parts that represent the opposite value structure, that which had to be rejected in the growing-up process. We call these parts the *disowned selves*.[1] Each of us has a surprising array of disowned selves. Learning about these selves is an important part of personal growth.

Let us look at how the protector/controller operates in the life of the child. Tommy is two years old. He is playing with his building blocks in his room, when his one-year-old brother Jerry comes into the room and wants to play with Tommy's toys. Tommy does not want him there, so he pushes him away and Jerry starts to cry. Their mother comes upstairs and tells Tommy he must learn to play with his brother, whether or not he likes it.

Tommy's basic feeling is that he'd like to punch his brother in the nose, but his protector/controller takes in the information from his mother and translates it into a formula for behavior. It now says to Tommy something like this: "Tommy, whatever your feelings about your brother, it's clear to me that your mother is going to give us a lot of trouble if we're not nice to him. It hurts too much to have your mother angry with us; it feels better when she loves us. So let's be nice to Jerry. You can hate him on the inside, but don't show your feelings directly anymore."

The protector/controller does not speak literally in this way at very young ages, but by the time we are adults, the voices of the selves are quite well-defined and it is relatively easy to talk directly to them. Such formulations are fairly typical of them.

We want to make clear that the development of this protector/controller is a major part of the development of personality. It becomes what we call the *acting ego*. It encourages other selves to develop and support its aims and aspirations. It sets the tone and the value structure of the

---

1. Nathaniel Brandon is credited with originating this concept in his book, *The Disowned Self* (New York: Nash Publishing Co., 1972. New York: Bantam Books, 1973).

personality. In the case of Tommy, it would encourage the self that has to do with "pleasing." Later, its emphasis would change and it would encourage the self that had to do with becoming ambitious and being successful and making large sums of money. This ambitious self grew in response to Tommy's father, who encouraged his son to be the best in everything. Tommy's father was fond of saying, "There are winners and losers in this world, Tommy, and I'm proud to see that you are one of the winners."

The protector/controller is a major part of the primary self system. Tommy grows up to be an aggressive and quite successful lawyer. His primary selves are associated with success, ambition, money, and rationality. These selves regulate his life and determine the way in which he sees himself. Tommy behaves well toward people—his pleaser sees to that—but he needs to be in charge and to control people. He may know that he is this kind of person, or, more likely, he may be unconscious of the fact.

The Disowned Selves

Each of the primary selves has a complementary disowned self that is equal and opposite in content and power. Tommy has identified with being an aggressive and ambitious type of person. In the service of power, he has disowned his vulnerability and his ability to communicate his neediness because, to the power sides of his personality, this is a sign of weakness. The opposite of his ambition is a disowned beach bum self that loves to be lazy and not do anything. Because this is so disowned in him, he often speaks proudly about his inability to unwind when he is on vacation and notices that when he does finally unwind, it is about time to return home. We will see shortly how important the understanding of these primary and disowned selves are in understanding our relationships.

Projection

Throughout the course of this book we shall see many examples of the relationship between primary selves and disowned selves. For the moment, it is important only to become aware of the fact that there lives within each of us a multitude of disowned selves, rejected parts of our inner family that most of us know nothing about. These selves remain in our unconscious, waiting for a chance to emerge and have their needs and feelings considered. Although they are unknown to us, they often have a surprisingly powerful impact upon our lives.

Those selves that are unconscious in us are automatically projected onto another person or another thing; our inner pictures are literally projected upon the other person as though the other person were a screen. These projections act like a bridge that extends out from us to meet that other person. It is one of the significant ways in which we make contact with other people in the world. Let us look at how this works.

John is an engineer who is successful in his work and who lives very much identified with primary selves associated with rationality, adventure, and travel. In the growing-up process he shunned the softer and more vulnerable parts of himself. His father was a strong, rational type, and the softness and femininity of his mother became increasingly alien to John, in large measure because he saw her as such a victim to his father. John is surprised to find that he is constantly falling in love with women who are very feeling-oriented, very feminine, and, as he would describe them, very soft.

Falling in love is, to a large extent, the projection of our unconscious selves onto another person. All of the softness and sensitivity that lie within John as disowned selves are projected onto these women. Sally, his latest love, has an additional feature; she is spiritual, an area of life that John has never touched and about which he has considerably negative feelings. Although John finds himself arguing with Sally for hours at a time about her spiritual viewpoint, he loves her deeply and is at some level fascinated by her unfamiliar way of looking at life. It is his own unconscious, then, that draws him into the relationship to Sally, via the mechanism of projection. By projecting these unconscious contents onto Sally, John has the chance to realize them in himself, if he uses their relationship as an opportunity to grow.

Sally grew up in a family where she was raised to be a loving daughter; all intellectual pursuit and personal achievement were discouraged. Finding the proper husband and raising a family were all her family encouraged. She got the message from her parents, over and over again, that she was very special and some man would be truly lucky to have her.

Sally's primary selves were loving and pleasing and caring. Her disowned selves were her rational and analytic mind, and her drive for professional achievement. We can easily see how these qualities in her unconscious would be projected onto John, while his opposite selves would be projected onto her. This kind of mutual projection is the natural start of many relationships, but it can be become damaging when we do not understand how it works.

These mutual projections can bring with them much richness when we see that they represent a natural tendency toward growth, a direct and exciting path for our evolution of consciousness, a chance to integrate unconscious material into our own lives.

Sandy worships his boss. He sees him as wise, fair, powerful, intuitive, sensitive, and godlike, the father he always wanted and never had. Then Sandy and his wife are invited to the boss's home for dinner. Sandy is horrified to find that his boss is henpecked, ridiculed, and seemingly ineffectual in the home situation. His idol has crumbled. The strong father he always wanted is no longer there for him.

This crumbling of our heroes generally happens when

we have projected too much power and authority onto them. But this kind of projection is a natural act, occurring constantly in our relationships. It is an integral part of our own personal development because it is through this projection that we can gain back our own power, the power that resides in our disowned selves. If we understand something about disowned selves and projection, then we can learn much from these projections and we have a better chance of reclaiming these selves.

Projection Onto Objects

Projection can occur in relationship to a person or it can occur in relationship to an object. Ralph bought an old army jeep for a considerable sum of money. He spent a fortune fixing it up and when he drove it, which was quite infrequently, something invariably went wrong. In addition, it was an extremely uncomfortable car in which to sit. His attachment to the jeep felt unnatural; one might almost say he felt possessed.

This is a feeling that often is experienced by people who are experiencing strong projections onto a person or an object. A few years before he bought the jeep, Ralph had accepted a major position with an international manufacturing firm. He worked very long hours, and his job was with him constantly. His primary selves had always had more to do with work and power. Playfulness and fun had always been a more disowned system of selves; with the responsibility of his new position, they became totally disowned.

What happened next? The part of him that knew how to be playful and adventurous had been projected onto the jeep. The extent of his possession by this vehicle is directly proportional to how strong the playful and adventurous selves are in him and how strongly they are disowned. The moment that he experienced these disowned selves within himself, through Voice Dialogue, the fascination with the jeep dissipated.

Whenever someone feels "possessed" by another person or thing we know automatically that the person or thing is carrying projected disowned selves. Much of the buying that people do is based on projection. All kinds of disowned energies are seen in bracelets, necklaces, dresses, cars, and boats. Used with awareness, such purchases can open us to new experiences and new possibilities.

Disowned Selves and Our Judgments

If we have grown up more identified with those selves that are associated with personal power, it would be most natural that we would disown the selves associated with vulnerability and neediness. Our acting ego would be identified with power. This means that in the course of growing up we have learned that vulnerability is something bad, something to be mastered. The power side judges vulnerability as something negative and, with time, an automatic shut-off valve comes into operation whenever vulnerability is experienced. When we meet someone who is more identified with vulnerability, our power side (which is our acting ego) tends to judge or react negatively to that person although at the same time we might feel a strong attraction to the person. The basic rule of the psyche can be expressed as follows:

> *The people in the world whom we hate, judge, or have strong negative reactions toward are direct representations of our disowned selves. Conversely, the people in the world whom we overvalue emotionally are also direct representations of our disowned selves.*

This psychic law has immense consequences in the realm of human relationships. Let us look at some examples to see how it operates in a more specific way.

Jane has grown up in a family where her natural sensuality had to be disowned. When she was a little girl, her mother was extremely critical of her whenever she danced in a sensual way, and especially when she acted sensually in relationship to her father, with whom she had a particularly strong bond.

Jane eventually married, but she had no awareness of the degree to which her own sensual nature was locked away. One evening she and her husband went to a party. There she saw a woman close to her own age who was a pure "Aphrodite" type (in Greek mythology, Aphrodite was the goddess of love and sensuality). This woman had had several drinks and was flirting outrageously with several men, who were happily flirting back.

Jane was revolted by this display and said to her husband: "That is the most disgusting sight I have ever seen!" What had happened? Watching this woman activated those selves in Jane that are related to her sensuality. Once those impulses began to emerge from within Jane, another self, based on her mother's rejection of sensuality, came into operation to suppress them. The name we give to this inner voice of the mother is the "introjected mother." The introjected mother blocks these impulses within by judging or attacking the person outside who carries the impulses.

The more powerful the affective reaction we have toward the other person, the stronger is the power of the disowned self. In this example, Jane's strong reaction indicated the presence of a powerful disowned sensual self. If Jane understood the basis of her strong negative reaction, what a marvelous opportunity she would have to reclaim this very basic part of herself.

Sherry works in an office, and she hates her boss. She describes her as domineering, power hungry, and unfeeling. Sherry had a mother who fit this same description. Very early in life, Sherry vowed she would never be this way, and she began disowning the part of herself that had to do with power and domination. In their place as primary selves appeared her very caring and loving nature. Now, whenever she was around anyone who carried her disowned attributes, Sherry became unbearably irritable and critical.

If Sherry understood the issue of disowned selves, she could have realized she was reacting, not to a person, but to a part of herself buried deep within; she could have used the opportunity presented by her boss as a challenge for her own personal development.

Disowned Selves in Relationship

Thus far, we have been discussing a number of very basic psychic laws.

1. *For every primary self with which we are identified, there are one or more disowned selves of equal and opposite energy.*

2. *Each disowned self is projected onto some person or some thing.*

3. *The people and things of the world that we reject, hate, and judge, or, conversely, those we overvalue, are direct representations of our disowned selves.*

4. *As a corollary to the third law, each person we judge, hate, reject, or each person we overvalue, is a potential teacher for us, if we can step back and see how the basis of our reaction is a disowned self of our own.*

5. *So long as a self is disowned within us, we will continue to repeatedly attract that particular energy in our life. The universe will bring us the people we judge, hate, and resent over and over again until we finally get the message that they are reflections of that which is disowned in us. Or, in contrast to this, the universe will bring us people whom we find marvelous and irresistable, people who make us feel inadequate, inferior, and unworthy. This will continue until we realize that these people are merely showing us aspects of ourselves that we have disowned.*

Some Examples of Disowned Selves in Relationship

George saw himself as a scrupulously honest businessman, but he had a strong dishonest streak in him that he had always denied. This disowned dishonesty led him to become involved in a business venture with a man who was fundamentally dishonest and cheated George out of a good deal of money. His denial of his own inner psychopath (and we all possess such "selves") made it very difficult to acknowledge the reality of this behavior in his business partner.

Even after it happened, George had a difficult time accepting the reality that he had been cheated. This disowning of one's own dishonest self is one of the reasons why so many people get cheated so easily.

Steve was a lawyer who was committed to being a loving human being at all times. He totally rejected the idea that any form of darkness existed in the world. In his business life, he got involved with strong criminal elements that almost destroyed his career.

The denial of the dishonest and criminal parts of themselves led both Steve and George into destructive situations. That is the paradox of disowned selves: we are drawn to the very people who carry these "unacceptable" qualities for us. This holds true whether the "unacceptable" qualities are good or bad; it applies to the persons we overvalue as well as those we despise. Life will constantly bring us face to face with people who represent our disowned selves, until we begin to reclaim these selves.

Bonding Patterns in Relationships

If two people in an ongoing relationship understand something about their primary and disowned selves, there is a much greater possibility of working out difficult and repetitive conflicts that arise between them. Let us look at some examples of how this works.

Larry and Janice have been married for five years. Larry is a meticulous, rational, ordered, and controlled person. His disowned selves are the opposite of each of these systems.

Janice carries most of his disowned energies. She is easygoing and does not care if the house is messy. She does not make up lists of things to do. She is feeling-oriented, with a very strong sensuality and sexuality.

Larry and Janice were passionately drawn to each other, but now they are beginning to have some difficulties. They have two young children, and Larry does not like to come home to a messy house. He begins to pick at Janice. Why can't she be organized and neater? He feels irritable and is beginning to sound more like a critical father than a husband and partner.

Janice is defensive. She begins to feel like she is back in her parental home, where her father carped at her constantly about her lack of order. Since she could never please him, no matter how hard she tried, she had stopped trying.

A new pattern has begun to emerge between Larry and Janice, particularly with the advent of their second child. Many of the selves that he saw as cute and sweet before have now become annoying to him. He finds himself becoming attracted to other women. He begins to think about having an affair. Neither knows what is happening; they feel miserable and disappointed and seem unable to deal with each other in any kind of creative fashion.

If we approach this from the standpoint of the disowned selves, we begin to get a partial picture of what is happening. Larry and Janice have both married their disowned selves, without knowing or understanding the real implications of this act. This is, in our experience, fairly typical. It is strange, in a way, because couples like Larry and Janice will often talk to each other and to other people about how different, how opposite they are in so many ways. So long as the bonding patterns remain positive, there is generally not too much difficulty. Once they become negative, it is no longer fun and the bonding wars begin in earnest. Let us look at what this looks like in a diagrammatic form.

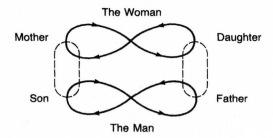

A Male-Female Interaction

In this diagram we see the basic male-female bonding pattern. The mother side of the woman is bonded to the son side of the man (the M-S axis), and the father side of the man is bonded to the daughter side of the woman (the F-D axis). This diagram illustrates the basic bonding pattern that exists in all male and female relationships before the development of any kind of awareness. It is a normal and natural process. It cannot be eliminated, nor would eliminating it be desirable; these bonding patterns contain much life and vitality. They often provide warmth and nurturing. The problem is that without awareness they are very likely to turn negative. In addition, the two people miss what is possible in the interaction of two aware egos.

In the early years of the relationship between Larry and Janice, these differences did not matter. Their bonding patterns remained essentially positive. With children, something began to change. Janice and Larry both felt somewhat overwhelmed and vulnerable, but neither of them was aware of these feelings. Janice let herself go a little more than she had before and, as the pressure grew, her inattention to details became even more pronounced. Larry, in turn, was more anxious with the added responsibility of a second child. He began to work harder as a way of balancing his sense of vulnerability. He needed order even more strongly as a way of handling his anxieties about money and the responsibility of a larger family. As he contracted more and more, he went into a role more aligned with "negative father" than "husband." Janice reacted to her sense of being overwhelmed by resorting to her primary selves as well. She became less and less concerned with what was happening. Thus, they began to push one another more deeply into their primary selves, making it more and more difficult to embrace one another's way of being. This is fairly typical of what happens in relationship when such conflicts begin. Both individuals tend to become more extreme in their identification with their primary selves.

To summarize what we have so far discussed, we refer to this way of being locked into each other in a relationship as a negative bonding pattern. *The term "bonding patterns" in relationship refers specifically to the activation of parent/child patterns of interaction between two people. These are normal and natural configurations that exist in all relationships.* This bonding can develop between any two people, whether they be male/female, male/male, or female/female. *The catalyst for all negative bonding patterns is the activation of the disowned vulnerability in the two people.* In this case, the arrival of the children made both Larry and Janice feel a bit overwhelmed and, therefore, vulnerable. *The fuel for these bonding patterns can generally be found in the mutuality of the disowned selves that exists between two people.* This keeps the bonding pattern burning bright and strong.

To analyze a negative bonding pattern in a relationship, one looks for the following:

1. What was the ignition point or catalyst? How was the vulnerability of the two people activated? Where are they feeling insecure, overwhelmed, or otherwise vulnerable?

2. What are the disowned selves that each carries for the other? What is the fuel that keeps the fires burning?

3. What are the actual selves that are involved in the bonding, i.e., the mother and daughter selves in the woman, and the father and son selves in the man?

With Janice and Larry, we have seen that the catalyst was the vulnerability cued off by the arrival of the children and the pressures this brought with it. The disowned selves then provided the fuel to keep the negative bonding pattern alive. Larry and Janice were opposites in many ways, as we have seen. He identified with his rational mind and his need for control of all details in his life. Since he disowned his own feeling and more "laid back" selves, and Janice carried them, her "laid back" behavior became one of the fuels for their bonding pattern. It became the substantive content for the judgmental father that was alive in him and waiting to be activated by the right circumstances. On the other hand, his anxious son, which had initially been activated by the demands of fatherhood, now felt even more panicked by the appearance of Janice's judgmental mother.

On her part, Janice disowned her more rational and orderly self and prided herself on her "laid back" approach to life. Earlier in their relationship, Larry's orientation to details was charming. Now, however, her judgmental mother began to feel critical of this behavior. Larry's need for control became the substantive content for her judgmental mother and it fueled her part of the bonding pattern. Janice also began to feel less sexual toward Larry. As his judgmental father emerged, Janice became increasingly angry and rebellious, moving into her rebellious daughter self, much as she had with her own demanding father. So we see with Janice how her disowned selves became the fuel for the mother/daughter aspect of herself that was waiting to be activated in the relationship.

It is interesting to note that our bonding patterns are very similar to the kinds of patterns that have existed in the past with our own parents or siblings. We literally re-create our past. We re-create what we had with our parents and/or siblings and what they had with us, or we go to the opposite extreme and rebel against the way they were with us. In this example, Larry had begun to criticize and judge Janice in the way his father had criticized and judged his mother. Janet responded as a hurt and then a rebellious daughter, just as she had with her own father. The bonding pattern then was between the judgmental father in him and the rebellious daughter in her. At some level we always have the reverse pattern in operation, even if it does not show itself at first glance. In this instance, it was Janice's judgmental mother that was bonded into Larry's anxious son, much as Larry's real father (who had been extremely judgmental) had bonded into this anxious son in Larry when he had lived at home. Diagrammatically it would look something like this:

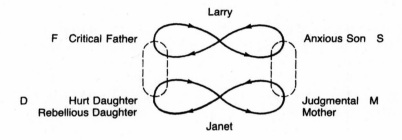

Larry and Janet-Negative Bonding

We would like to point out that bonding patterns of this kind that exist *without awareness* can cause all kinds of misery and mischief, but there is something that can be done about them. *These bonding patterns represent the primary reason for the disintegration of the romance and the feelings of love in relationship and often are responsible for the destruction of a positive sexual experience as well. It is our view that they represent a primary reason for many of the misunderstandings and disturbances in relationships and friendships.*

This book is basically about the understanding of these bonding patterns. These patterns operate in many of our interactions with people, but they are of particular significance in our most important ongoing relationships. In these long-term situations they tend to become much more ingrained and uncomfortable, motivating us to figure out what is happening to us. As we learn about these bonding patterns and develop an awareness of how they operate, we often find that we can use this information to move ahead and into a period of accelerated personal growth. As for the bonding patterns themselves, although they do not disappear, they become less deadly, and there is an introduction of greater humor and understanding into the relationship.

The Consciousness Process

When we talk about personal growth, we like to describe it as the consciousness process; sometimes we talk about the evolution of consciousness. The idea of process is a very important part of our understanding and thinking. Consciousness is not a static thing; one never becomes "conscious." One is always in the *process* of becoming more conscious. What, then, are the elements that constitute this process? We see three different levels of activity that are essential to our way of thinking about consciousness. In listing them in the order of levels 1, 2, and 3 we are not implying that one is better than the other. The levels are for purposes of clarification only.

Level 1: Awareness

The awareness level of consciousness is what many people have in mind when they talk about consciousness. It is often referred to as the "witness." Awareness gives one the ability to step back from one's mind, one's emotions, one's body, and one's spiritual nature and to simply view them in a totally dispassionate way. In the awareness level there is no attachment to the outcome of things. It is not an emotional state, nor is it a rational state. It has nothing to do with control.

For instance, if the awareness level is operating within us (Sidra and Hal) at the present moment, we do not have to be identified with the ideas that we are expressing, because our awareness is separate from these ideas and our feelings about them. It frees us from the necessity of forcing our ideas upon you and allows us to focus on the clarity of the presentation rather than being concerned with how the ideas will be received. This automatically frees us from the negative aspects of our inner critics, perfectionists, and pleasers and we are able to write. You can see from this example what a wonderful gift awareness is and you can well understand why it has been the basic goal of so many spiritual and meditative systems.

The awareness level of consciousness allows each of us to step into a certain moment of time and witness what is there. We must realize, however, that this awareness level is not an action level. Since it is not attached to the outcome of things, but is simply there as an observing point of reference, some other part of us must deal with the information made available to us through our awareness.

Level 2: The Experience of the Different Selves

The second consideration in our definition of consciousness has to do with experience. Awareness, we have seen, is a point of reference; there is no intellectual or emotional involvement. A full definition of consciousness must also include the experience of the different parts of ourselves and their experience of the world around us. Without experience, we would lose our sense of who we are as human beings in the world and would lose the excitement and intensity of life.

For example, we might have an experience of our anger or our jealousy, or love, or pride, or religious ecstasy, or any of a host of possible emotional reactions. If we only become *aware* of things, then we lose our relationship to the amazing variety of experience that is available to us. If we only *experience*, without awareness, then we remain forever identified with our experiences and cannot separate from them. We could drown in our feelings.

For example, let us say that John feels very jealous of his girlfriend when they are at a party together. If John tries to *become aware* as a way of transcending the experience of jealousy, then he loses the reality of the experience of jealousy. If, however, he remains jealous and angry without awareness, then he remains locked into the *experience of jealousy* with no possibility of behaving in a different way. If he goes into an awareness level and transcends the anger, or tries to, then he loses the power and vitality of this very significant emotion. What he does with this anger and how he handles it is something that John has to deal with. Each of us must learn to embrace all of the selves. As we continue to learn from our experiences and to embrace our many selves, we find that life has more options than we had ever imagined possible.

Awareness and experience, therefore, are two inseparable partners in the way we look at the consciousness process. Each has its job to do and, together, they bring us much richness. Even together, however, they are not sufficient. Another partner is needed in this business consortium. Who or what is going to evaluate all this information and experience? Who or what is going to take advantage of all this awareness and experience and decide what to do with it? This brings us to level 3 of our definition of the consciousness process.

Level 3: The Aware Ego

The concept of the ego has been around for a considerable period of time. Historically speaking, the ego has always been defined as the executive function of the psyche; it is the decision-maker. From the standpoint of an individual who is oriented more toward the rational self, the idea of the ego as making choices and executing decisions is very appealing. A person's life must have someone in charge. Otherwise it is like driving in a car with a vast multitude of selves fighting with one another about who gets the wheel. Historically speaking, it is the job of the ego to be in charge, to drive the psychological car.

What we discover about the ego when we first work with the different selves in people is that it is really an *operating ego*, an ego that is basically the self or selves that the people happen to be identified with at that particular time. So, to go back to the example we have been using, if you have been raised in a family in which rationality has been emphasized, and if you are identified with this self, then what you will think of as your ego is basically your rational self. Without an awareness of this, you may feel, quite contentedly, that all your decisions come out of clear choice and free will when, in reality, your rational self is making all your choices under the guise of an ego. To repeat, we call this kind of ego an *operating ego*.

What we propose, then, is the idea of an ego that is constantly in process. It is forever taking in the information provided by the awareness level of consciousness. It is forever dealing with the experience of the different selves within and how these selves are reacting to, and experiencing, the world without. We call this the *aware ego. It is very important to understand that when we use this term, we always are referring to a process and not an entity.* There is no such *thing* as an aware ego. There is only an individual ego that is attempting to evaluate the constant input of awareness and experience and thus be in a better position to make more effective choices in the world. Thus, an ego that is becoming increasingly aware helps us to stay young and alive, allows us to continue to grow, and keeps our options in life open.

The aware ego has another quality that is very important. It has the ability to embrace and to hold the tension between totally different selves. As a matter of fact, it is only an aware ego that has this capability. Let us see how this works. Mary is a 33-year-old mother of three children. She is happily married and enjoys her family life and children. The problem is that she has begun to suffer from migraine headaches. Her nights have become increasingly restless and she recalls dreams of being chased by dark figures. She finally seeks professional help to alter this pattern.

In her earlier life, Mary was a bright student and had already begun graduate school when she and her husband met. They fell in love and were married, though she had some misgivings about the possibility of losing her career. Her mother strongly influenced her to get married and have a family. This fit in well with the part of Mary that really feared the challenge of a graduate program and all that would entail. The part of her that wanted the career went underground. She was no longer carrying the tension of opposites.

It is not the decision of what to do in life that is an issue from our perspective. The issue is whether we can carry the tension of the opposites no matter which way we go. In Mary's case, it would have meant that she maintain a connection to the voice in her that wanted a career. Instead, getting married was no longer just a question of marrying the man she loved. It was also a solution to her conflict about a professional life, and so it became a way out for her.

Since both Mary and her husband wanted children, it was not long before the children came and now, ten years later, she had three of them. Mary was a good mother, and her sense of who she was as a person became increasingly identified with her role as mother. The selves that had been operating in graduate school, that wanted to become a clinical social worker, gradually disappeared from her awareness. They became, in effect, disowned selves. Mary's ego was now fully identified with those selves that were related to being a mother. These selves, in fact, had become her operating ego.

Another cluster of selves seemed to disappear at this time as well. Mary reported that the sexual relationship in the marriage had all but vanished, although she was quick to point out this was no problem for either her husband or herself. It just did not seem to matter. They were very happy with their family, which gave them much comfort and joy. They were leading just the kind of life that they had always dreamed about.

Mary was bright, and she was able to see the extent to which the non-mother selves in her had been eliminated or disowned. As an awareness level began to develop, she began to see the extent to which her ego was identified with the mother role. As her ego separated from the mother role, she also began to be aware of, and to experience, a whole new group of feelings and thoughts that were quite contrary to what she had known before. She became aware of how often she felt anger toward the children. She became aware of the part of her that wanted to forget everything and just go to Greece for a year. She began to feel how dead the marriage had become, and suddenly sexuality became a serious issue for her. She became aware of the part of her that wanted a professional life, that was tired of spending her days at home and driving carpools and cooking meals.

Mary had indeed begun to develop an aware ego, and now she was able to begin to embrace two very contradictory and powerful systems of selves within her. One system of selves wanted her to remain home and raise her children and give them the fullest possible mothering they could get. This part said to her: "Too many women choose career over children and the children always have to pay the piper. Your father left you when you were quite young and your mother had to go out to work, so you know the trauma of a mother-less home." On the other side of the conflict were the selves that spoke as follows: "We are bored out of our minds with this stultifying life that you are leading. You have 'put in' eight full-time years of mothering and it is time for a change. We are not telling you to get rid of the children, but just to begin to take our voices seriously and start to think about our feelings and needs. Otherwise we are going to make you good and sick and you'll be forced to deal with us from a hospital bed. We cannot stand this anymore."

What does Mary do with this conflict? She learns to carry it. She learns to live with opposites. She needs to disengage from both sides and learn to use both kinds of energy in her life. She has two totally opposite people living inside of her and she has to be able to stretch out her arms to embrace both of them. She has to learn how to live with discomfort, how to *sweat*. When one embraces opposites, one sweats. The greater the power of the aware ego, the more the sweat. It is only an aware ego that can learn to live with seemingly irreconcilable opposites.

Let us return to the three levels of our definition of consciousness. We have awareness, the experience of the different energies and selves, and an ego that is in an ongoing process of becoming more aware and is constantly evaluating experience so that it can make more effective choices. If we believe in this definition, then it has far-reaching consequences. It means, for example, that we are all just fine the way we are, so long as these conditions are met. It means that if Mary gets angry at her children, and she has awareness and an ego that is taking advantage of the experience, then that is the process of consciousness.

Many people who are interested in the consciousness process and who strive toward personal development have a concept in their minds about the way that they should be in life. Their goal is usually a state of tranquillity and awareness. It is often the case that when they experience strong affective states like jealousy or anger, guilt is experienced because these are not tranquil or aware feelings. An inner voice then criticizes them for feeling this way. If, however, there is no need for this kind of perfection, as in our way of viewing the consciousness process, then this inner critic is remarkably stilled and everything is fine just as it is.

More About the Aware Ego and the Issue of Surrender

For people on a spiritual path, the concept of the ego is a distasteful one. "Ego" is seen as worldly, prideful, rational, arrogant, power-oriented, and most certainly not surrendered to any kind of spiritual power. So it has happened in many spiritual traditions that people are taught to eradicate their egos because only then can they be truly on a spiritual path.

From our perspective, the ego to which they are referring is not the "process of the aware ego," but rather the operating ego. It is what is commonly *called* ego but which is, in fact, *the primary selves with which the ego has been identified.* Since these primary selves have been largely identified with rationality for many centuries, it is no wonder that an ego that has been identified with these selves rejects the non-rational aspects of reality and would be a hindrance to anyone on a spiritual path. It is, therefore, perfectly understandable why spiritually oriented people reject the concept of ego as too limiting.

Furthermore, for those dedicated to the eradication of the ego, there is a feeling that the identification with ego leads one down a blind path that removes one from one's spiritual origins. This argument conveys the idea that the ego must give way to a deeper part of oneself that is less concerned with worldly things. It sees the ego as interfering with the ability to experience divinity or to surrender to a spiritual path. This deeper self, they feel, needs to gradually become the prime mover in life and as this process takes place, the ego gradually relinquishes its role and fades into oblivion.

What we are talking about in our view of the consciousness process is the *aware* ego. It is the task of this aware ego to embrace all of the different selves without being identified with any of them. It is only an aware ego that can do this. *An aware ego is surrendered to the process of the evolution of consciousness.* It accepts the sacred task of becoming aligned with all of the various energy configurations that constitute who we are as human beings. Since this is a process and, so far as we can determine, there is no ultimate final condition of consciousness, *the surrender is to the process itself.*

Since the aware ego is surrendered to the *process* of consciousness, it is open to the total range of possible experiences. It embraces them all, positive and negative, "acceptable" and "unacceptable," without being married to any of them.

This surrender of the aware ego to the process of the evolution of consciousness has certain consequences. It means that we cannot be selective in what we embrace or do not embrace. *An aware ego can be selective in what it does ultimately with the different energies. It cannot be selective about its willingness to embrace all of them. The choice lies in the subsequent action taken, not in the embrace itself. Embracing a part does not mean becoming it.* Instead, it means honoring the part, as one would honor a god or goddess. In our viewpoint, the aware ego seeks to honor all the different selves and energies exactly as though they were gods and goddesses.

We then might try to give a name to this new kind of surrender, and we believe quite profoundly that it is a new kind of surrender, one that leads to a new kind of renaissance person. We might say that this surrender to the process itself, and the requirement that we gradually learn to embrace all the selves, is a surrender to Spirit with a capital *S* rather than a small *s*. We might even say that it is a surrender to a much wider and more comprehensive vision of Spirit than anything we have known before. We might see it as the surrender to an intelligence that lives within the unconscious itself, an intelligence that has as its goal the evolution of consciousness in the human species. We might say that it is all of the above.

If we wish to surrender to the process of consciousness, we must surrender to it in all its complexities and contradictions. If we want to be loving human beings, we must learn to love our own wolves and jaguars and snakes and dragons, our stupidity and irritability and weakness and vulnerability and darkness as much as we love our loving and rational, competent, caring, and light-oriented selves. To have as a goal the honoring of all the energy systems that exist within us is a highly devotional act. By whatever name we call it, it is indeed a new kind of surrender and a new kind of awakening. It is this kind of surrender and this kind of process that opens us to relationship as one of the most powerful teachers on the planet. Now let us turn to the most basic aspect of this teaching, the introduction to the vulnerable inner child who we see as the doorway to our unique and, at the same time, universal soul.

2

Vulnerability: The Key to
Intimacy in Relationship

The Importance of Vulnerability

As we have clearly stated in the previous chapter, the entire development of personality, or primary selves, is aimed at protecting one's vulnerability. When we discuss falling in love, in the next chapter, we will show how the actual act of falling in love allows the vulnerable child, the carrier of this vulnerability, to surface and to make an intense contact with another human being without the usual protection of these primary selves. This ability to be vulnerable with one another, to allow the emergence of every feeling, thought, and reaction and to cherish all of them, makes the process of falling in love a wonderful experience. *It is one's vulnerability that makes intimacy in relationship possible, and, conversely, it is this same vulnerability and apparent lack of power that the primary selves most fear in relationship.*

Just as it is the inclusion of vulnerability in relationship that allows intimacy, so it is the disowning of this vulnerability that later destroys intimacy. Over the years, we

32

have found that in our own relationship, and in the relationships of those around us, *it is disowned vulnerability that is the catalyst of all bonding patterns that, in turn, destroy true intimacy. When we disown our vulnerable child, we do not attend to it properly. Since it is imperative for this child to receive adequate care, it will look elsewhere and bond into the people around us, requiring them to provide the care that is otherwise lacking. We will not be aware of this process because we do not know about our vulnerability. So, in an entirely unconscious fashion, we are automatically drawn into powerful parent/child bondings over and over again.* Sometimes these bonding patterns feel positive, and sometimes they feel negative. These bonding patterns have been introduced in Chapter One, and, since they are of the utmost importance in relationships, we will devote much additional space to them in the following chapters.

How might this denial of vulnerability and subsequent bonding look? Let us say that Larry and Lauren are driving to dinner. The night is dark and stormy and the road winds along a cliff. Larry is driving, as usual, but tonight he is tired, the day has been difficult, and he is feeling uneasy but does not know why. Larry, however, does not know about his vulnerability and so he pushes his feelings of uneasiness down, moving instead into his judgmental father self and becoming more and more critical. He questions Lauren about what she has done during the day and becomes particularly irritable when he discovers that she spent two hours at lunch with a friend. "Why don't you take care of business, why are you wasting time at lunch when you haven't finished our tax preparation yet?" he finally shouts at her. And off they go. An evening that was supposed to be a pleasure turns into a miserable affair with both people feeling dreadful and neither knowing what has happened.

What actually has happened is that Larry has denied his vulnerability, and his needy child has automatically and unconsciously bonded into Lauren. This child needs her to be taking care of Larry even though Larry is not aware of it.

Larry has also bonded to Lauren from his judgmental father, who criticizes her for not meeting the needs of this child. How might this be different if Larry were aware of the needs of his child and had some choices of how to behave? Larry would be in touch with his vulnerability; he would know that he was tired and uneasy. He would then be in a position to take some action through an aware ego. He might suggest that Lauren drive to dinner so that he could relax; he might suggest that they go someplace closer to home; or he might just take the opportunity presented by being in the car alone with her to talk about his unhappiness and exhaustion. In this way, he would be dealing directly with the underlying vulnerability and taking responsibility for the care of his own vulnerable child.

Caring for this inner child through an aware ego gives a feeling of real strength. It represents, in our way of thinking, real empowerment. When the aware ego is caring for the vulnerable child, there is no longer the need to rely solely upon the automatic protective devices provided by the primary selves, even though this has given a sense of security in the past. Nor is there the need to rely upon others to assume responsibility for this child. *It is important to know that each one of us is ultimately responsible for parenting the vulnerable child within. When we are caring adequately for our own vulnerability, we are in a position to relate deeply and effectively to others.* When we do not care adequately for our own vulnerable child, it will seek this care elsewhere and bond in deeply and unconsciously to the parental side of others. In order to care for the vulnerable child, we must understand how it operates within us.

The Vulnerable Child

Vulnerability is much maligned in our culture. It has been seen as a womanly trait, unworthy of a man or of a truly successful and admirable human being. For the more spiritually oriented, it has been viewed as a lack of trust in one's spiritual commitment, a serious impediment to growth and transformation. To be identified with one's vulnerability can, indeed, make one a victim to the world.

We have all met people who have been identified with their vulnerability. They react with an excess of sensitivity to all situations and are powerless to either protect themselves or to get their needs met appropriately. They are quintessential victims, constantly being hurt or exploited by others. They have no awareness of their own power; therefore they have no power in the world.

We do not in any way feel that elevating one's vulnerability above all other selves is a good idea. However, we will state categorically *that for any relationship to remain alive and intimate, to grow and to deepen, the awareness of one's own vulnerability is absolutely necessary.* The aware ego must have at its disposal an awareness of the feelings, perceptions, and needs of the vulnerable child in order to be able to relate to another in a genuinely intimate fashion. It is this child that carries the deepest feelings in our hearts and that can recognize the feelings deep in the hearts of others. It makes a contact that is palpable; it creates a physical warmth between two people that is totally delightful. This child cannot be fooled by words or by reason because it responds directly to energies or feelings. This child is also unbelievably sensitive to the slightest indication of disapproval or abandonment; it is likely to react catastrophically to its fears of either.

If there is no access to vulnerability, then our lives are dominated by our primary selves that, in turn, are relating to the primary selves of others. We are well protected, but alone. The sadness of this condition was beautifully conveyed in a dream that was told to us rather wistfully at a workshop: "Hal reached into my bag and pulled out a book of poems. He started reading them aloud. I remember thinking that they weren't mine. This made me feel "safe" but it also made me feel sad. Since my vulnerability wasn't revealed, he couldn't disapprove of me—but he couldn't really approve either."

The vulnerable child is the actual self within each of us that carries our emotional reality. It is this child who remembers all of the experiences that have touched us deeply or have caused us great pain. Its memories are far more complete than those that are usually available to our primary selves. It often has full recall of specific traumatic experiences that have been otherwise repressed.

The child will also remember beautiful love-filled experiences. Alice's vulnerable child, for instance, was able to sing the hymns that she had sung years before with a beloved grandmother, long since dead. The loss of this grandmother was so painful, and the reality of living with an emotionally withholding mother was so unpleasant, that Alice's vulnerable child was completely disowned at the time of her grandmother's death. A cool, rational, judgmental mother took over, which buried Alice's vulnerability completely. With this as her primary self, Alice experienced only irritation and discomfort with hymns whenever she heard them and spoke disparagingly of the singers. She took great pains to avoid any contact with what she termed "fundamentalist Christians" and she did not even like Sundays.

When we talked to her about disowned selves, Alice was skeptical that she could have disowned anything to do with hymns; the whole matter seemed quite foolish to her. Later, when we then contacted her vulnerable child, the child tearfully reminded Alice of the great peace and happiness that she had experienced as a very young child, when her grandmother played the piano on Sundays and they sang hymns together. Once Alice realized that she had, indeed, disowned something that had to do with hymns, her inner child was in a position to bring back to her some of the lost happiness and warmth of her childhood, the memories of singing with her beloved grandmother. She had also moved from an operating ego dominated by her "judgmental mother" self to a more aware ego that, for the first time, had some access to her inner child.

Disowning the Vulnerable Child

Most of us have learned early in life to disown our vulnerability. Instead, we have identified with other selves that bring with them more power in the world. It is usually in relationship, whether a love relationship, a therapeutic relationship, relationship to a guru, or a very deep friendship, that there is a chance to learn for the first time about this very sensitive vulnerable child that lives deep within each of us.

In our travels around the world, we have had the good fortune to meet many beautiful vulnerable children within people. It is amazing to see how similar they are, despite great differences in culture. The neglect these vulnerable children have faced as the result of being disowned is graphically illustrated in the dreams that often follow the first awareness of their existence. Nothing gives the picture of the disowning and neglect as well as these dreams, which have come from all over the United States, from Australia, Israel, England, Ireland, Wales, Switzerland, and Holland.

In the following dream, Jim's disowning process is shown quite clearly. Jim sees his vulnerability as ugly, something to be resented, and, most of all, something that threatens to keep him from an adult sexual relationship:

> I came into the room and there was a big double bed covered with white sheets. I was planning to get into it. I saw a little bed next to it, and on the bed was a heap of white bed clothes with a little bit of hair sticking out. I went over to look at it and saw an ugly little child, 4 or 5 years old. I didn't want to go near it, and I resented it. I felt that it was going to keep me from getting into the big double bed.

Jim was so disgusted by his own vulnerability that he would have nothing to do with it. He had identified strongly with his achieving selves and pushed himself in his work to such an extent that he finally became ill. It was only through illness that Jim's vulnerability could be expressed and that he could finally allow himself to be cared for. He found he enjoyed his convalescence very much, because it was the first time he had been allowed by his overactive pusher to stop and rest.

For people like Jim, there is a distinct negative reaction to the first discovery of the vulnerable child. Steve felt much the same as Jim did about vulnerability. After contacting his vulnerability for the first time, he had the following dream:

> I'm in a houseboat. I know that this is the life that I've created and I am happy with it. I like being strong and self-sufficient. As I realize that I really don't want to change my way of being in the world, I see two men, a large strong man and a smaller one who is naked and has a beautiful body. The large one tells the other one to run. As he begins to run, his beautiful body becomes deformed. Then he has a heart attack. He continues to run as he was told, and then he becomes sick and throws up. Now I think that he may be too damaged to live.

In this dream, Steve is given an objective picture of his reaction to the discovery of his vulnerability. His dominant power side, in the form of a strong pusher, holds on to its primary position, refusing to allow the newly discovered, smaller, less powerful, but beautiful side to live its life undisturbed. In the disowning process, the powerful pushing self drives this less powerful part until it is almost completely destroyed. This pushing self continues to hurry Steve mercilessly through life, keeping others at a safe distance. It has absolutely no time for relating.

Using Voice Dialogue to
Gain Access to the Vulnerable Child

In contrast to these examples, there are other instances in which the vulnerable child is greeted with deep love and much joy. During one of our workshops we introduced the topic of vulnerability and then demonstrated the Voice Dialogue method, using the technique to speak in front of the group with someone's vulnerable child. This served to trigger the inner child in many of the other group members. That night, Jeanne, a participant in the workshop who thought that she was in touch with her own inner child, dreamt she received a message that her "grand" child was in trouble:

> When I heard where he was, I went to the woman's house to get him. The woman showed me a big fat baby covered with Band-Aids. She said to me: "We're not worried about the child's physical condition, but we had no idea who he belonged to. He's been hanging out here all the time." I replied: "But I don't understand this because he's been with me all the time." Then I knew that I was going to have to take him with me and find out why he was trying to get away from me. I realized that I was going to have to talk to him, and that he was scared to death that he wasn't going to be cared for.

Jeanne, realizing that she needed to contact her vulnerable child, requested a Voice Dialogue session. She contacted a very touching and extremely sensitive little girl who had experienced a good deal of pain in life. It seemed that Jeanne was in touch with other aspects of her childlike nature—her magical, sweet, imaginative, playful parts—but not the part of herself that carried her vulnerability and neediness. We will now give a brief section of the interaction with this child to show what a vulnerable child sounds like when it speaks directly.

> FACILITATOR (to Jeanne): I'd like to speak with your little girl, the one who's scared, not the playful one who has just been talking to us.

Jeanne, who has had Voice Dialogue sessions before, moves to another chair and turns her back to the other people who are watching her.

CHILD: (Looks up at the facilitator and does not speak.)

FACILITATOR: It's kind of hard to talk, isn't it?

CHILD: (Nods her head and says nothing, but maintains eye contact.)

FACILITATOR: Well, you don't have to say anything; I'll just sit here and keep you company. Do you want me to keep talking to you?

CHILD: (Nods again.)

FACILITATOR: O.K. You look pretty little to me. Jeanne is pretty grown up, and she always knows what to say and how to make people feel good. But you're different, aren't you? (Child nods again.) You look pretty quiet to me.

CHILD: I am quiet. Noise scares me. Big people scare me. You're okay; you talk very softly. But I can't look at the other people. They scare me.

FACILITATOR: (Nods and remains silent because the child is talking.)

CHILD: My Mom scared me a lot. I used to be scared a lot when I was little because it was noisy a lot. I like quiet. My ears hurt when it's noisy. My heart jumps around a lot too.

At this point, the facilitator goes into an exploration of Jeanne's childhood. There is great emotional intensity to the interaction. At first the vulnerable child is quite tense and holds onto her knees tightly, looking intently into the facilitator's eyes for any sign of disapproval or inattention. She is extremely sensitive to any distraction. Gradually her grip loosens as she tells about the things that had frightened her during Jeanne's childhood. The experience is quite moving, as buried, emotional memories surface. Then, after quite some time, they turn to more current issues.

FACILITATOR: (Begins to question what aspects of Jeanne's current life bother the child.) So, you don't like it when there's a lot of noise and you're really sensitive when people are angry or rough. What else don't you like in Jeanne's life right now?

CHILD: I like to be in my own room with the door closed, and I like to open it to let my friends in one at a time. She never closes her door. I don't like it when she leaves her door open and the others always come in. I don't like it when they mess up her room. I don't like having children in her room. I only like grownups there, because they're quiet and they don't mess things.

FACILITATOR: I see. So you don't want other kids around a lot.

CHILD: No I don't. I like her grandchild, but I don't like all the other kids she takes care of. I only want her to take care of me. I'm tired of her taking care of everybody else. She promised me that when her own kids were grown up, we would have fun together and she would stop worrying about everybody else. Now it's time. I want her to spend time with me and buy me pretty things and brush my hair and let me just sit by myself and look out the window at the trees and dream and not do anything. And I want to sing.

I like her daughter. I want to go for a walk with her and just hang out, and not run errands and not talk about important things. And I don't like it when people leave her their children to take care of and they go off and have fun. And I get scared when they get annoyed with her if she's too busy to take care of the children.

I don't feel good when people don't like her. It makes me feel terrible. I want everybody to like her. But I want her to tell them to take care of their own children anyway! Even if they do get mad at her. She's not their Mom.

The facilitator continues to talk with Jeanne's child for about two hours, and the child relaxes more and more. She literally blossoms like a flower. Jeanne becomes quite fond of this child, as does everyone else who was observing this particular Voice Dialogue session. That night, Jeanne has a second dream:

First I dreamt that my "grand" child was lying down all wrapped up tightly. The next moment, I saw her lying there unwrapped and beautiful, with her blonde hair lying on the pillow. I loved this child dearly and I wanted her to be as happy as she is beautiful. I awoke feeling very happy.

Jeanne's discovery of her vulnerable child meant a great deal to her. She felt much love for it and welcomed it as a beautiful addition to her life, as her dream demonstrates. She began to pay attention to the child immediately and to meet its needs, rather than to automatically meet the needs of the people around her and neglect her own, as she had in the past.

The Neglected Vulnerable Child

We have collected many dreams that poignantly illustrate the neglect of the vulnerable child. They were dreamt by people who had come to our workshops and had just become aware of this part of themselves. The unconscious then picked up the process and showed them quite clearly how they had disowned their vulnerability.

Many of these dreams have a similar theme. The dreamers go off to work, or to play, or to be with others and suddenly remember that they have forgotten the child or children who were left in their care. In each case, the dreamer experiences a feeling of panic and a rush to reclaim the child, with the fervent hope that it had not died or suffered permanent damage. The child is usually in sad shape—hungry, cold, neglected, dirty, frightened, or ill. In one dream, the child had been transformed into a little animal. Happily enough, the child is usually not dead and, in most instances, there is hope for its eventual recovery.

Marie's dream is typical of this category:

> I am in a hotel room, up on a high floor. It is warm and comfortable and luxurious. I hear a small sound and look out onto a very narrow balcony. There is a little girl who has been outside on this balcony for a long, long time. It is cold and raining outside, and she is freezing. I feel terrible because I know I was responsible for her and I'd forgotten about her.

Marie is a sophisticated, wealthy young woman who enjoys the good life. However, she has been cut off from her vulnerability since early childhood, because vulnerability is simply not a clever or elegant attribute and it was definitively discouraged in her social milieu. So she learned to live her life "high up" and sophisticated, and her inner child was left to freeze outside on the balcony.

Sometimes our vulnerable selves are relegated to a secondary status because they are not as exciting as our primary selves. They are overlooked at first, and eventually, as they continue to be pushed aside by our primary selves, they become disowned. After she was introduced to the concept of vulnerability in a lecture, Mandy had the following dream:

> All my parts (selves) are in a big room, talking and having a great time. They are all trying to get my attention; they are exciting and lots of fun. I love being with them. In the far corner, there is a small child who calls to me and says, "Please don't forget me."

This dream gives a clear picture of how the primary selves can easily distract us from noticing our more vulnerable, sensitive selves. Here, after listening to a discussion of vulnerability, Mandy suddenly notices her own vulnerable child, which has been sitting unnoticed in the corner until now.

The Resilience of the Vulnerable Child

The vulnerable child appears to be small and weak, but we have found that its role in everyone's life is amazingly powerful. The more that one knows of this child and the more that one integrates it into daily life, the more conscious one's behavior becomes. We have found that in most instances when people have tried to contact this child, even though it might have been disowned for a lifetime, the child is quite ready to be heard. It has proven surprisingly resilient despite years of neglect.

Where there has been serious emotional damage, it is this child that needs to be healed, and an extended period of psychotherapy may well be required. However, when this inner child has been disowned under ordinary circumstances, it frequently recovers from its period of disowning, bounces back to health, and begins to bring riches with it almost immediately.

The sturdiness of the vulnerable child was clear in George's dream. After being introduced to the concept of vulnerability when he read our book, he dreamt:

> There was a baby stuck up in a tree screaming and crying and it wanted to be taken down. I was too scared to go up to get it. It kept calling to me, but neither I nor anyone else with me went to get it. Finally, it jumped out of the tree. I felt badly that I hadn't gotten to it sooner, and I ran over to see if it was okay. Its feet were bruised, but it was all right otherwise. I held it and comforted it.

In this dream, the unconscious helps George to reach his inner child. He is still identified with his primary selves, who have as their aim in life the disowning of this vulnerable child. Once the initial contact is made, there is a chance for the aware ego to take over and to perform the natural act of comforting and caring for the vulnerable child in an appropriate fashion.

Repetitive dreams about neglecting babies and young children often indicate that vulnerability has been disowned, as we have shown earlier. Mildred, who had repetitive dreams of this type, began to take her vulnerability seriously. She experimented with a variety of psychological and spiritual methods and learned to care for her vulnerable child through an aware ego in an appropriate fashion. She said of her later dreams,"I have been noticing a change in my dreams. I still have a baby whom I've forgotten about. I used to dream that I left it on a shelf and then I would panic and look for it and find it half starved. These dreams repeated themselves and each time the baby has been less neglected. Last time I dreamt that I was breast-feeding it and it was fat and happy." These dreams clearly reflect how Mildred's change in consciousness and the new way in which she is honoring her vulnerability has resulted in the gradual healing of her vulnerable child.

Caring for the Vulnerable Child

Once the vulnerable child has been discovered and the issue of vulnerability in relationship has been opened up, there is a chance for real change and sustained growth. We would strongly suggest that the vulnerable child be addressed directly through the Voice Dialogue technique, which has been briefly illustrated earlier in this chapter (a thorough presentation of the technique can be found in the companion book to this one, *Embracing Our Selves*). However, any approach that enables one to directly contact this child or to become aware of one's vulnerability will be of great help. In her book, *The Power of Your Other Hand* (Newcastle Publishing Company), Lucia Capacchione has developed a technique of journal writing, using the non-dominant hand, which provides an excellent means of accessing the vulnerable child. Whatever the means of contact, it is important to become aware of what is happening to one's inner child, so that the aware ego can utilize the information to care for the child in an appropriate fashion.

This last point is important enough to bear repeating. *When we disown our vulnerable child, we do not attend to it properly. Disowning this child does not make it go away! Since it is imperative for this child to receive adequate care, it will look elsewhere and bond into the people around us, requiring them to provide the care that is otherwise lacking. We will not be aware of this process because we do not know about our vulnerability. In an entirely unconscious fashion, we will be automatically drawn into powerful parent/child bondings over and over again.*

We see many examples of this kind of bonding in our everyday lives. Perhaps the most common is the strong professional man who relates to everyone around him as the responsible father who is always available to help others and to care for their vulnerability. If he has no awareness of his own vulnerability, this professional man will bond strongly into someone who provides him with the same kind of care that he gives to others. The caretaker may be a nurturing wife, but often it is an office manager or secretary. This bonding will be particularly intense if the man is uncomfortably shy around people outside of his professional role, or if he feels inadequate in terms of general business knowledge and office procedures. He will feel helpless if his office manager or secretary must skip work for a day, since he depends upon her to deal with all the aspects of life that frighten him, like disciplining the other office workers or attending to his finances.

When this bonding is particularly powerful and unconscious, as is so often the case, this man who is the strong, supportive father to everyone else is the inadequate and compliant son to the caretaker's managing mother. When this bonding is in effect, this substitute caretaker can do whatever she wishes in the office; he will be powerless to stop her. He feels frightened of losing her and is helpless to ask her to change any behavior that might prove problematical. Since the woman is living out of her managing mother self and not through an aware ego, she can become a real tyrant in the office.

Many powerful women become involved in one disastrous love affair after another. Man after man disappoints them in their search for a loving and rewarding relationship. It is our experience that this, too, is often the result of disowned vulnerability. Since the powerful woman does not know about her own vulnerable child, it bonds into one man after another, trying to get its needs met. The primary selves of the woman are strong and independent. They would be

horrified to realize that underneath Wonder Woman is a
vulnerable little girl. Without this awareness, there is no
opportunity for a strong and otherwise sensible woman to
find out about her inner child, to honor it, to speak up for it,
and to go about meeting its needs in a thoughtful way. Her
neglected, needy child looks elsewhere for understanding
and bonds into the man, hoping that he will understand her
completely, do away with her yearning, and make her happy.
Since no one but herself can truly care for her vulnerability,
she is doomed to bond in as needy daughter to each man in
her life, and to be disappointed by each in turn.

The opposite situation occurs when one knows about the
vulnerable child and identifies with it completely. For such
people, the vulnerability is the primary self system and the
power selves are disowned. This is guaranteed misery. For
those who are totally identified with vulnerability, there is
only an endless parade of bondings in which one assumes the
victim role and is repeatedly victimized. For those identified
with vulnerability, strength always resides in the other
person, and there is complete dependence and constant
neediness. Although there may be a period of bonding into
the good parent in friends and lovers, this is usually not
permanent, and the bad parent exacts the payment for all
that the good parent has given, causing much pain and a
dreadful feeling of betrayal.

*As one gets to know about one's vulnerable child, it is extremely
important to keep in mind that indulging all its feelings is no better
than ignoring them.* One needs an adult around to care for the
child, an aware ego to make conscious choices that take its
needs into consideration but is not identified with these
needs or run by the child's fears and sensitivities. Otherwise
one is in the position of a parent who, when faced with a
weeping child, identifies completely with the child and
weeps with it. The parent, then, is in no position to offer
another perspective and certainly has no ideas as to how the
child might take care of its pain. The parent is in the same

position as the child, and there is no choice available to either of them. They must both remain in pain waiting for someone on the outside to intervene.

How can we take care of our inner children? The most important step in caring for the inner child is to recognize its presence and to develop an awareness of its particular personality, its needs, and its reactions. Once we know about the child and its needs and feelings, we are in a position to do something about them. We must learn to separate far enough from our vulnerable selves to realistically evaluate situations in which they have been activated, and then to speak up for them in an objective fashion, rather than to put them in a position of taking care of themselves. *This ability to be objective in considering the requirements and reactions of the vulnerable child represents a true position of empowerment. It is the most powerful way in which to move into a truly intimate connection with another person and to avoid the pitfalls of bonding patterns—or to gently extricate ourselves once these bondings have been constellated.*

We have found that people have evolved many ways of caring for their vulnerable selves. For most of us, one of the best ways to take care of our vulnerability is to be sure that we have a network of people whom we love and with whom we feel safe. In that way, our inner children receive nurturing from a variety of sources and always have a place to go when they need one. Also, it is important for most vulnerable children to have some space they can call their own, however small it might be. This would be a place that the particular child finds aesthetically pleasing and one in which it feels safe.

It is fascinating to speak directly to the vulnerable child and then to consider how to meet its specific requirements. If one is fearful of a long trip, there may be something special to take along to make things more comfortable. We know people who travel with favorite pillows, pictures of their families, favorite books, stuffed animals, or incense and crystals. One woman about to embark on her first business trip alone realized that her child was fearful of eating by herself in a restaurant. She was greatly relieved when she figured out that she could watch television in her room and order from room service. A man who was newly divorced discovered that his vulnerable child missed the smell of food cooking. He began to prepare meals at home and to keep food in his refrigerator so that his inner child would not feel so abandoned.

There are many ways of taking care of our vulnerable children. We must first learn to listen to them and to honor them, taking their input seriously *but not allowing them to tyrannize us or those around us*. We should be good parents to them, honoring them and helping them to move past their fears when this is necessary. This does not mean that we try to make them grow up. The vulnerable child remains a child forever.

Each of us must learn about and care for our own vulnerable child in our own particular way. After the vulnerable child has been contacted, it will often help in this process. It has been known to appear in dreams to give instructions regarding its care.

Sam had not known about his vulnerable child and had allowed his life to be run by his need to succeed and to impress others, even though this tendency to overwork could have resulted in illness or other damage to his body arising from constant muscular tension. Once he found out about his vulnerable child, Sam decided that he had to pay more attention to him and to take his needs seriously. He dreamt as follows:

> A child came into my house, a child that I knew was related to me. I knew that he had come alone across a busy street. I told him, "You must never come to me unescorted again." He had really risked his life to get to me and now he had to be more careful.

The change has come about and the growth has already started. Sam's unconscious took responsibility and began teaching Sam about his child and the risks that it runs. Sam realized that his disregard for his own physical health was truly dangerous and he decided to take better care of his body.

Before she knew about her inner child, Ann was very brave. She dared anything, laughing at danger and at the fears of others. As she contacted her inner child, Ann gradually became aware that it was not at all happy with this state of affairs, that it wanted her to be a bit more cautious, particularly where Ann's feelings were concerned. Although Ann was willing to "walk through fire" in her relationships, her child had other ideas. After she began to take the child more seriously, the Dream Weaver sent Ann the following dream:

> I (Ann) was taller and wore a long skirt. I was a classic maternal figure living in a beautiful house in the bush, amongst gardens. My house burned and I went in to get the baby, who was asleep. I picked up the baby and realized that although I could walk through the ring of fire, it would burn the baby. So I decided to stay inside the ring of fire. I found a crystal clear pool and got in with the baby. The baby continued to sleep peacefully as I waited for the fire to recede. As I watched, I noticed that the fire wasn't destroying anything. I was amazed.

We have found that if one cares for the inner child in this way in a relationship, there is time to sit still and work on the internal situation until some awareness is available, a certain amount of clarity is achieved, and the aware ego can make a more appropriate move. Then the fires can burn themselves out without doing any damage. It is the disowning of the child, the walking through the ring of fire without any awareness of the harm that is being done to the child, that alerts the defending primary selves and catalyzes the bonding patterns. Once the negative bonding patterns are activated, the fire *does* do damage.

The Role of the Impersonal Self
in Caring for the Vulnerable Child

One of the most important aspects of protection of the vulnerable child is a self that can be characterized as impersonal or objective. This self is clear-thinking, direct, and dispassionate, even in the face of the needs or the emotional reactions of others. It is often unavailable to women in our culture, although men usually have fairly ready access to it. Women have usually been trained out of their impersonality and, instead, encouraged to be emotionally available at all times, even when this interferes with their ability to evaluate a situation, determine their own needs and boundaries, and act effectively.

It is not unusual for a woman to have access to these impersonal energies at work but to be unable to utilize them in her more intimate relationships. If she is a teacher or a therapist, she may be able to use her impersonal energies to discipline pupils or to set limits, define boundaries, and contain the neediness of clients. The same woman, when dealing with her husband or her children, may lose this ability completely, responding instead in terms of their needs and feelings, without any consideration of her own.

Fran was this kind of woman. She had been raised by a seriously disturbed mother, a truly vicious woman. Because her mother was dysfunctional, Fran had to become the mother to her entire family at the tender age of five. She disowned her own vulnerability and instead identified totally with her internal "mother," which became her primary self. She was always available to care for the vulnerability of others with great love and responsibility. She desperately needed to be more impersonal and to set limits on what people could demand of her.

After working to develop the more objective side of herself, Fran had the following dream:

I was in a house with a lot of children. There was a group of
tall, tough men outside trying to get in. I wanted to run away.
There was a father there who was big and strong, with a tea
towel over his shoulder. He was taking care of the children. He
told those louts that they could come in, but they mustn't hurt
the children. You have the feeling that the father can take care
of things.

The father in this dream represented Fran's new way of
taking care of the children. He could protect Fran from the
"louts"; he did not need to run away nor did he have to go to
war with them. He could simply deal with them objectively
and with great impersonality, keeping them all, louts and
children, in their proper places.

As Fran, or any other man or woman, continues to
develop her objective self and separates from the personal
part of her that needs all relationships to be warm and close
and nurturing, she will have an increasing number of choices
in her life. She will be able to consider her relationships—
even the most intimate ones—with some degree of objectivity and will be able to factor in her own needs when
making decisions within the relationships.

An opposite example is that of the businesswoman who
has a very well-developed impersonal side that can deal with
all sorts of issues at work without becoming emotionally
involved with others. Her relationships at the office are
pleasant but not personal. She has no need to maintain
emotional contact with anyone, she does not need anyone's
love or approval, and, therefore, she can move ahead and take
care of business.

This same woman, in an intimate relationship where her
vulnerable child desperately needs to maintain intense emotional contact at all times, might well lose the protection of
the impersonal businesswoman self that functions so well at
the office. If she does, this straightforward, self-confident,
self-sufficient woman is likely to be overwhelmed by the
neediness, the fears, and the awkwardness of her vulnerable

child. She will then bond in automatically to others in a variety of unsatisfying ways. She might even become the complete victim in relationship because, somehow, she cannot bring to bear any of her impersonal objectivity when she is intimate.

Although women have traditionally been the ones to identify with personal, or loving and related energies, and men have tended to carry the impersonal, we have seen some change in this during the past 20 years. Men, too, are now encouraged to be more feeling and to exclude their impersonal selves from relationship. We have seen that the introduction of some impersonal elements into intimate relationship is extremely helpful, and we have emphasized this particular self because of its ability to help the aware ego in protecting and caring for the vulnerable child.

In this chapter, we have shown the importance of vulnerability in relationship and have introduced you to the vulnerable inner child. One of the most basic lessons of relationship is the development of a conscious relationship to this child. We have shown some ways in which people have learned this lesson. In the next section, as we begin to give examples of how relationship can be a teacher, we will show how the disowning, or denial, of this vulnerability triggers the negative bonding patterns that disrupt intimacy and cause untold discomfort in relationships. But first, we will speak of the initial phase of relationship, the period of falling in love, when the vulnerable child feels happy and safe.

PART II

Relationship as Teacher

3

Falling in Love

The beginning of a relationship is indeed a magical time of wonderful feelings, great excitement, and apparently limitless possibilities. This can be true of any relationship that touches our souls. It can be true of a romantic relationship, a friendship, a relationship with a teacher, therapist, or guru. It can even be true within families.

What happens when someone falls in love? As we have said before, people are made up of many parts or selves. But each of us has a specific group of *primary selves*—an elite ruling group. It is this group of selves that constitutes our personality as we and those around us know it. This group of subpersonalities, or selves, is led by the protector/controller, a self that has spent a lifetime figuring out how to get along in the world. This protector/controller has evolved a code of behavior that is appropriate to the family, the culture, and the subculture in which we have grown up. It has gathered about itself a group of selves that support it in its efforts to lead a safe life, a life that enables us to fit smoothly into our surroundings and that is approved of by other people who are important to us.

This group of primary selves helps us to fit into the world around us so that our sensitive, secret vulnerable child will, hopefully, never get hurt. Therefore, this group is usually fairly conservative. It is headed by a very careful protector/controller, which keeps its eye on family, friends, and work associates to check out which behaviors will be rewarded and which should be avoided. It gathers about itself other selves like the perfectionist (who knows how things should be done), the critic (who shows us where we fall short of the perfectionist's ideals), the pusher (who helps us to move along faster, always faster), the good mother or father (who makes sure that we take care of everybody else), and the pleaser (who does as others wish). These selves usually make up the elite group that dominates our lives. We *identify with* these selves; it is this group of selves which constitutes our personality as we view ourselves and as our friends see us.

As we have said before, for each primary self there is a complementary, or opposite, self that is *disowned* or kept out of consciousness. For instance, if our protector/controller is conservative and cautious, we might disown our gambler or our liberal. If we identify with our good mother or good father, we will disown our own selfish child. If we identify with our sensible, well-adjusted self, we will disown our emotional self. Our vulnerable child, the part of us that carries our vulnerability and sensitivity, is not only disowned but is usually hidden away someplace safe—like in a concrete bunker buried 60 feet beneath the cement basement floor.

When we fall in love, everything goes topsy turvy! Most of the protector/controller's carefully worked out rules get suspended. Somehow, our vulnerable child escapes from its "safe" hiding place and comes out to take a peek at the world that, for this wonderful period of time, seems safe enough and most definitely welcoming whenever the beloved is near. The usual crowd of primary selves loses its power and the door is left open for new selves to emerge. We go through our lives for a magical time, without our usual caution. We are able to see and hear things that we had never known before. It is as though we have entered into a new world.

The New World

When we fall in love with someone, a lover, a teacher, a therapist, our newborn son or daughter, suddenly the world is full of new possibilities. We notice a beautiful vista to the side of the road because our consciousness is changed. The castle may have been there all the time, but we never saw it before. We have a new lover and suddenly we notice the flower shops in our neighborhood. Our therapist tells us about the importance of dreams, and we notice that we dream every night. We have a baby and the entire world looks fresh and new. A beautiful song in the fifties put it quite well: "There were birds in the air but I never heard them singing, never heard them at all till there was you."

The world *is* actually new to us because we are literally perceiving it through new eyes. Until now, we have lived a life governed by a small group of primary selves; we have perceived it through their particular sensory apparatus, understood it to their way of understanding, and evaluated it according to their particular values. We have identified with them and their values, and their frame of reference has been ours. Now, as we fall in love, this balance of power is disrupted. These dominant or primary selves that have governed our lives lose power because there is little threat to our well-being. For the moment, we are not in danger of being hurt and our vulnerable child is happy and safe with the beloved. As these primary selves lose power, the complementary disowned selves emerge naturally. Let us see how this might happen.

Changes in Our Selves

When we fall in love, the pusher that usually sets our pace is overridden. Suddenly, everything that was ever so important can wait a bit while we spend hours on the telephone or squeeze out a few more minutes for a romantic dinner or find just the right gift for the beloved. We may discover, much to our surprise, that we have a Dreamer who likes to spend hours thinking lovely thoughts, or a Romantic who reads poetry, takes long walks, watches the sunsets, and engages in many other similarly non-productive activities. We may even discover a self-indulgent self that loves to spend great amounts of time and much money on non-essential items.

Before she met Bob, Susan's pusher was the general manager in her life, and Susan was careful to use all of her time productively. Then she fell in love. She now decides to take time from her busy schedule to go to the hairdresser, to shop, to have her nails manicured. She spends money on perfume and somehow finds the time to indulge in long hot baths. She discovers that she most assuredly has a luxury-loving self that had been totally disowned, pushed out of the picture by her ever eager pusher. Before she fell in love, Susan was totally unaware that any part of her might enjoy these activities.

When we are deeply in love, the critic, who up until now has evaluated our appearance and our productivity in life with a fairly jaundiced eye, suddenly seems to disappear. Instead, we look into our lover's eyes and see ourselves mirrored back in all our beauty. For this magical period, we are lovely just as we are, and whatever it is that we do is just fine. Even our usually unattractive idiosyncrasies become charming when mirrored in the eyes of someone who loves us unconditionally. As the critic loses its power, we are free to create, enjoy, explore, and feel. As we no longer feel the power of this critical presence in our lives, we can become more creative and more loving, to say nothing of less stressed!

Someone once said that the most beautiful songs that are ever sung are those sung to infants by their mothers, songs that will never be heard by anyone else. And this may well be true. Because when we have fallen in love with a child who in turn loves us unconditionally, we want to communicate with it from our very hearts, and there is no critic commenting upon the quality of this communication.

A woman in her late twenties, Mary has been doing a good but apparently uninspired job at her work. She falls in love and suddenly her work flourishes. She becomes relaxed, creative, humorous, and almost brilliant. Her critic has taken a back seat and no longer paralyzes her with self-conscious indecision. Mary has gained access to her natural courage and spontaneity and is able to use them freely without undue interference.

Somehow, when we are in love, the perfectionist becomes less important because now the world does not need improving. It is beautiful just the way it is. We look at it through the proverbial rose-colored glasses. We change our focus completely and even see the flowers growing on garbage heaps. We, too, are spared the perfectionist's scrutiny, and we can go about our lives in a more relaxed fashion.

For example, everything had to be done just right for Esther. She could not leave anything half done or undone. She could not go to bed at night until all the dishes were done, the latest bills were paid and the checkbook balanced. Of course, her house was always spotless and her office well-organized. She never left anything on her desk at night. Nothing was less than perfect. Then Esther fell in love. Everything in her life began to look pretty good to her. Now, not only does everything seem pretty fine just the way that it is, but her priorities have begun to change, and her perfectionist seems to have disappeared completely. Her new boyfriend, Andrew, is more relaxed about everything and she, too, has become more relaxed. Her own inner "Andrew" has emerged. Esther now works well but not compulsively. She is able to view her life in a more balanced fashion, approaching tasks in a relaxed manner. For the first time, she has some choice about how, and when, she wants to do things.

Surprisingly enough, when we are in love, we no longer need the pleaser because everything we do seems to please our beloved and we are free to be totally ourselves. Now we are able to trust ourselves and our own tastes and desires, since they are accepted so unconditionally by the person who is most important to our vulnerable child. We might even develop a selfish self. This is particularly likely if we have had a tendency to spend a good deal of time in the good parent or the pleaser. Since we want to spend much of our time with the loved one, we will, of necessity, do less for other people in our lives and will have to say no.

As a devoted and dutiful daughter, Angela has learned to ignore her own needs. Then she falls in love. She is no longer able to put her mother's interests ahead of her own because this new relationship is too important to her. Therefore, she must separate from the dutiful daughter part of her and claim time for herself, thus incorporating her selfish part.

When we fall in love, the rational self, which has been evaluating life and setting up expectations that are sensible and realistic (in its view), begins to look too narrow in its approach. Up until now, it has decided which feelings are appropriate in any given situation, rejecting those that seem immature, volatile, or, worse yet, overly optimistic. As we experience the rush of excitement that often accompanies falling in love, we may find that the sober view of the rational self recedes into the background, and in its place we find a cock-eyed optimist.

Laura had learned not to expect too much from life. Her childhood had been difficult and her mother had disappointed her with great regularity. Even when she first met Larry, she was afraid to let herself go completely. But, somehow, his love and persistence worked their way through her reserve and touched her deeply. She fell in love. To her great surprise, she found that she no longer analyzed every aspect of their relationship. Instead of her usual cautious and rational approach, she was excited and optimistic. As her optimist emerged, Laura realized that she had a wonderfully spontaneous sense of humor that had never before appeared in her life.

The emergence of these disowned selves brings with it a double gift of psychological energy. First, as we have seen, each new self brings a new kind of energy into our lives. The brain research reported by Michael Gazzaniga suggests that there are actually different brain modules for different sub-personalities or selves.[1] *Thus, we are likely to be activating unused portions of our brains with each disowned self that comes to the surface. Secondly, an enormous amount of psychic energy is used to keep disowned selves disowned or repressed. The process of disowning or repressing is an active one that robs us of vitality that can be experienced in other areas of our lives.*

Thus, as Laura brings forth her optimist, she not only adds to her life all the humor, hopes, and enthusiastic perceptions of the optimist, but all the energy that was required to keep these perceptions from awareness. Each time in the past that Laura's optimist might have said, "That's great!", her rational self would have had to use an equal and opposite energy to push it down and replace that thought with, "Don't get too excited, you'll just be disappointed. Things never work out."

The Gift of Selves

What a marvelous gift of selves is brought by the beloved when we fall in love! This gift is brought in two ways. The first, as we have already seen, is the natural release of a

1. Gazzaniga, Michael S. *The Social Brain*. New York: Basic Books, Inc., 1985.

number of disowned selves when the status quo is disrupted and our primary group of selves is relieved of some of its power. As the primary self loses power, the complementary disowned self usually emerges.

The second way in which we gain access to new selves begins with the psychological mechanism of *projection*. We literally project upon the other person qualities that may or may not be his/hers. When we first fall in love, these projections are all positive. The beloved represents much that we want to be. As we see these attributes in the other person, the selves within us that would match these attributes become activated. It is as though an energetic resonance is set up and the two energies become synchronized.

At first, we are not aware that we have the matching self within us. We may feel simple and see our beloved as wise; we may be fearful and see the other as brave; we may feel mundane and see the other as romantic and creative.

The beloved can be anyone, not just a lover. When this process of projection occurs in a patient-therapist relationship, it is called *transference*. The therapist or teacher is seen as having a wide variety of attributes that mirror the selves that are not accessible to us because they are either unconscious or disowned.

An *unconscious self* is just that—a self that has not been made conscious—while a disowned self is one that has been actively pushed out by an opposing primary self. The disowned selves that are projected upon the beloved are often emotionally charged. There is a reason that these selves have been disowned and the primary selves have had an interest in keeping them disowned. We want to be safe in life, and these are the selves that might be unsafe. That is why it takes a powerful experience like falling in love to upset the orderly progression of our lives. Let us see how this process works.

Eleanor had been raised by very rational parents who were not affectionate. She often felt rejected and learned at an early age that if she cared too much, she was likely to get hurt. Eleanor learned to bury her natural exuberance and eventually became an extremely successful businesswoman. She was proud of her level-headed, sophisticated, and rational approach to life. She never took emotional chances; in fact, she disowned her emotionality completely. She hid her vulnerability and lived a life that was self-sufficient, taking very good care of herself in every area of life. She was even sure to have many boyfriends, so that she did not get too involved with any one of them.

When Eleanor fell in love with Steve, everything changed. Steve was an unabashed romanticist who worshipped intense feelings. She found this aspect of him absolutely charming; in fact, it was the quality in him that most attracted her.

In order to build a bridge to him and to give him the depth of emotional contact that he required, she needed to gain access to her own buried emotions. She found that she had within her an emotional teenager, a part that had never been allowed in her life before. She discovered that she was surprisingly reactive to Steve, happy when he called, miserable when he did not. She knew what her feelings were and she loved to talk about them. She loved being in love. This previously disowned teenager brought with her a new aliveness that had never before been a part of Eleanor's experience of life. She was not always happy, but her life was truly exciting and intense. It was the kind of life that she had so often envied in others.

When John was a child, he played make-believe games and wrote short stories. He was a dreamer, and he loved to create for the sake of creativity. His parents were hardworking people who saw no use in his daydreaming. They would chastise him for being foolish and wasting time. He was told that he was to be productive at all times. He was teased and embarrassed whenever he spent time daydreaming and, fairly soon, his creative self was disowned. John learned to work hard; he got the recognition that he wanted from his parents, and he soon forgot all about his childhood enjoyment and the many happy hours he had spent playing pretend.

When he fell in love, John chose a writer who specialized in fiction. He had no thought that he could write, too. Instead, he idolized her and her ability to use words and to create. As she wrote poetry to him, he longed to speak to her in her own language, to connect in a deeper way. He wanted this so badly that he no longer felt the embarrassment about his creativity that he had learned in his family home. His own creative self re-emerged and he began to write poetry and short stories. He then remembered the happiness he had felt as a child, and he was able to regain access not only to this happiness but also to the poet's view of life that was naturally his.

A woman of the 1950s, Barbara learned that in order to be taken care of, she had to disown her own strength and her natural abilities in the business world. She did this so well that she identified fully with her helpless child and married a strong, very domineering man who demanded complete control of her life. After they were divorced, she fell in love with Andy, a sensitive man who greatly admired her sophistication and power. In response to his encouragement, she was free to become as powerful as she wished, and she developed a most impressive businesswoman self that brought with it many rewards.

Thus far, the selves we have examined have been disowned selves. Another way in which we encounter new selves during the process of falling in love is when we bring forth a previously unconscious self. We do this when we develop a completely new self through the contact with the beloved. Because we love and admire the other, we are willing to learn something new or to try out a different way of being in the world. We may eat sushi for the first time. We may have been brought up in a completely disorganized family, and when we fall in love, we might well choose someone who knows how to organize life. We learn the necessary skills from the beloved and add them to our own repertoire. It is not that we disowned sushi, we just hadn't tried it; it is not that we disowned organization, we just did not know how to organize.

As an academician, Georgia did not have much time for physical activity in her life. She met Brad, who was an avid scuba diver, and he encouraged her to learn to dive. She earned her certification with her usual thoroughness and was extremely happy with her new skills.

Ernie had been raised in a working class home and had not been exposed to the cultural activities available in his city. He entered therapy with a female therapist who at some point mentioned that she had gone to a symphony concert. Although he had never done so before, Ernie decided to attend a concert, too, in order to see what it would be like. He enjoyed himself thoroughly and discovered a love of classical music that remained long after the therapy ended.

Keeping the Gift

These gifts are priceless. Each new self adds immeasurably to our enjoyment of life and to the intensity with which we live. Of greatest importance, each new self enhances our consciousness and represents a step forward in our personal evolutionary process.

Unfortunately, many of us confuse the gift with the giver of the gift. When the falling in love part of a relationship is over—or, for that matter, when the relationship itself is over—we return the gift to the giver. We feel that somehow these new selves are not truly ours, and we go back to our old patterns of living. Sadder still are those amongst us who retrench further and allow even greater power to our previously dominant selves, because they have "proven" to us again that we need to go through life according to their rules, so that we will remain safe and avoid disappointment.

If, instead, we treasure the gifts that have been given in a relationship, if we treasure the new selves that have emerged during this magical period, then the relationship has added something new to our lives. In this way, each relationship leaves behind an expanded consciousness and the gift of new or enhanced selves.

4

Where Has Love Gone?
Bonding Patterns
in Primary Relationship

What is it that happens to a perfectly beautiful relationship that suddenly causes the end of intimacy and understanding? One moment, one is in love, the beloved is a compassionate, loving human being and the world is harmonious. The very next moment, everything is out of balance and dissonant. The beloved suddenly looks like a childish fool who will never learn appropriate adult behavior, or like an unfeeling, critical, demanding parental type who thinks she/he knows all the answers to life's questions. The overwhelming feeling tone in life changes from one of optimism and grace to one of disappointment, despair, and the distrust of all relationships. One simply knows, at a very deep level, that this is yet another proof that relationships cannot work, that they all turn out the same, and that nobody is to be trusted. Obviously, this relationship, too, is doomed to failure; actually it is probably over already, because nothing could survive the current set of dreadful feelings. These catastrophic feelings are the definitive signs that the negative aspects of a bonding pattern have taken hold in the relationship.

The reader was introduced to the idea of bonding patterns in relationship in the first chapter of this book. In Chapter Two, we examined the concept of vulnerability. We saw how critically important it is to be in touch with the vulnerable aspect of our beings, and how vulnerability is at the core of most of the difficulties in relationship. We moved then to a discussion of falling in love and how this changes our lives. In the next chapters we will concentrate more fully on the nature of the bonding patterns themselves. It is the work with these bonding patterns and the eventual understanding of how they operate in our lives that enable us to learn from each of our relationships and to use them to help us move forward.

To help you to understand bonding patterns, we have chosen a wide range of examples to present to you. They portray many different kinds of conflict situations that occur and re-occur in relationships. Our discussion attempts to show how, in each case, the primary selves and disowned selves are playing off against each other between the people involved. From our perspective, the awareness of bonding patterns, and the experience of the different selves that we identify with and disown, is the key to the development of more conscious personal relationships. Let us now observe the dance of the selves and learn how they move with each other to create the marvelous music of human relationship.

The Ignition of, and the Fuel for, Bonding Patterns

By definition, a bonding pattern in relationship is the activation of parent/child interactions between any two people, that is, the bonding of the child selves of one to the parental selves in the other. For example, the mother self of a woman may lock into the son self of a man, or a father self of a man might bond into the daughter self of a woman. These patterns occur in primary relationships, both heterosexual and homosexual, in familial relationships, in friendships, at work—in short, anywhere two or more people are interacting with one another.

This process is much the same as the bonding process that occurs between the infant and its parents. The original, and prototypical, bonding pattern is between the infant and its parents. It is natural, instinctive, and unconscious. It is the way in which we are able to give and receive nurturing. Thus, it represents a most basic unit of human interaction. The bonding patterns that we set up in infancy and early childhood remain with us throughout our lives. They represent our primary way of making contact with others, until awareness enters the picture.

Bonding patterns are perfectly normal processes that come and go constantly in all relationships. When they are operating in a positive manner, they tend not to be a problem. For example, a woman might live the mother role in her relationship to her friend, who lives the daughter role, and for many years (perhaps even for a lifetime) there might not be any conflict between them. This bonding pattern then represents the form of the relationship.

However, one of the interesting things about maintaining the positive aspect of these roles in a bonded relationship is that the negativity in the relationship is generally disowned and tends to remain unconscious. If something happens to trigger one of the couple, the disowned negativity of many years may erupt, either or both women become very angry, and neither of them knows quite what has happened. It very often feels in this kind of situation like being kicked out of paradise. There is an almost unbearable feeling of betrayal when a positive bonding pattern is broken, because it involves the loss of a nurturing parent.

Thus it is that bonding patterns generally come to our attention when things start to go sour with them, when they begin to break up. The problems inherent in positive bonding may be quite obvious to friends of a couple, but the individuals involved in such a relationship are generally the last ones to know that they are living in such a pattern. The negativity and pain that we experience when things go sour in relationship lets us know that we have been in a bonding pattern of which we were unaware. Working through the negativity can then become a real education for the two people, once they can step out of the rage, judgments, righteousness, and victim status that characterize negative bonding patterns.

We start with the basic premise that bonding patterns are a natural part of all relationships and that in their positive form they generally go unnoticed. As people become more aware in their personal lives, living these bonding patterns full-time becomes less acceptable. More and more people today are not satisfied with this kind of relationship.

Awareness is a reference point that is outside the actual system of the bonding pattern. The aware ego has one foot inside and one foot outside the system of the bonding pattern. Let us look at a diagram of the bonding pattern with awareness and the aware ego included:

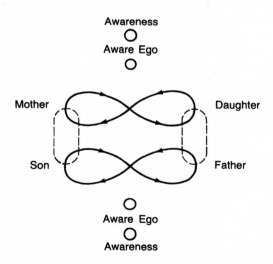

Bonding Pattern with Awareness and Aware Ego

Bonding Patterns
with Awareness and Aware Ego

The awareness level allows us to witness the different patterns that are occurring between ourselves and others. The aware ego is able to utilize awareness and also to experience the actual bonding patterns. Once the aware ego begins to operate, we have some small measure of choice in regard to the bonding interactions. An aware ego does not stop bonding patterns; nothing can stop them. But the aware ego can modify them and, more important, can learn how to use them in a way that is creative in the process of personal change and growth. Last, but certainly not least, an aware ego usually has some sense of humor and some distance from the abject misery that the negative bonding patterns invariably bring with them.

When problems begin in a relationship, there is usually an ignition of the negative aspect of a bonding pattern. Once this pattern is ignited, there is generally a fuel that provides the basis for its continuing emotional intensity. *As far as we can determine, the ignition system for these negative bondings is some injury to the vulnerable child. Its feelings are hurt; it feels abandoned; it feels endangered; it feels left out; it is fatigued or hungry. When we are unaware of these feelings, that is, when we are not conscious of this kind of uneasiness or injury, then we move psychologically into some kind of power place and identify ourselves with a powerful self.*

So we see that vulnerability is the key to the understanding of these bonding patterns. The vulnerable child provides the ignition and a good part of the fuel for the emotional charge. There is additional fuel, however, that operates to maintain the fire and heat of negative bonding situations. *The additional fuel is the system of disowned selves that operates between two people in a relationship.* Whatever we disown is carried by another person. Those things that we resent, reject, despise, and judge in other people are direct representations of our disowned selves. These disowned selves that we carry for each other in relationship become the basis for much of the passion that we see in negative bonding patterns. Let us see how these considerations apply directly to the realm of personal relationships.

Disowning Vulnerability

Bea and Al have gone to a party and both have had a fair amount to drink. Al flirts outrageously with a woman there. When they come home, Bea is quite withdrawn and very angry underneath. She also feels foolish, because she has no respect for jealousy as a natural feeling. She is very much identified with the idea of being a free spirit and allowing Al to be whatever he needs to be. This is the first time in her life that she has ever felt jealousy with a man, and it is anathema to her because it smacks of possessiveness. Possessiveness is the last thing she wants to be accused of in her relationships!

From our perspective, there is yet a deeper issue that lies underneath the jealousy, and that is her vulnerability. Bea does not like to be vulnerable. She will go to any lengths to avoid it. To admit jealousy is to admit vulnerability. Her primary selves do not permit this to happen, so whenever she feels vulnerable, her power sides come into operation. Her power voice is her free spirit voice. It says to her, "You have to be strong in relationship. You and Al both have the right to be exactly who you are and you need to support each other in this process. If Al is turned onto another woman, so be it. That is what he needs to do for himself and you need to support him in that process. Jealousy and vulnerability are signs of weakness and show a problem with self-esteem. They have no place in a good relationship."

On the other side is Bea's vulnerable child. The feelings that come from this place are very different. The child would say to her something like this: "I feel bad. I love Al and I feel terrible when he flirts with someone else. I feel like he's abandoning me."

The child side of a person is needy and vulnerable and, as we shall see over and over again, is typically disowned in personal relationships. By being disowned and not being allowed the chance to be expressed in relationship, this child side goes more deeply underground, where it becomes increasingly needy and vulnerable and begins to exert a powerful effect on one's life. When this child becomes too powerful in this disowning process, it can take over the personality and produce a person who is totally vulnerable and is always the victim in relationships.

There is another self in Bea that her power side does not like at all, and that is the rage that lies underneath her jealousy. Generally speaking, vulnerability lies at the deepest level, and rage is really a reaction to the vulnerability. The rage side of Bea, were it given the chance to come out, would attack Al or scream at him or let him know in some powerful and overt way that she was enraged with him. Bea's power side is inexorably rational, as we have seen. Anger is considered unseemly behavior and is definitely taboo. The problem in this interaction is that her power side is not able to handle the situation. Her vulnerability is too great and so is her rage. The more she has to block and disown these feelings the more crippled she becomes and the more she falls into the victim role with Al.

On a theoretical level, Al is committed to the same view of relationship that we have described above. His flirtatiousness at the party came out of his commitment to the idea that in a relationship, both people must be able to do what they need to do for themselves. In this instance, the flirtatious behavior was supported by a considerable amount of alcohol, and now that the whole thing is over, Al feels guilty toward Bea. If there is anything in the world his power side hates, it is to feel guilt in relationship to a woman. What is worse, Bea has gone into a withdrawal. At first this withdrawal has to do the victim daughter who feels hurt and betrayed. Soon, however, this shifts into the negative mother who withdraws her energy and becomes quite punitive. All of this happens without a word being said.

Al and Bea are now moving very quickly between father/daughter and mother/son in their bonding patterns:

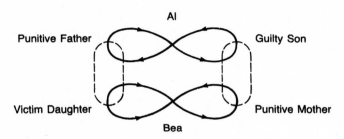

Al

Punitive Father   Guilty Son

Victim Daughter   Punitive Mother

Bea

Bonding Pattern of Al and Bea

Al is shifting from the guilty son to the punitive father who resents feeling guilty, and then back to his guilty son as Bea becomes more punitive and withdrawn. Basically, he feels terrible. His guilty son just knows that he has done something wrong and is truly terrified of Bea's punitive mother. Deep within herself, Bea may intermittently experience a twinge of the discomfort of her vulnerability, hurt, and jealousy. However, this cannot be handled because it is all disowned, and so back she goes into the withdrawn and punitive mother. This is the dance of relationship, the dance of bonding. All this is going on between Bea and Al and not one word has yet been spoken. These shifts occur with amazing speed, which is one reason why it is so difficult to identify the patterns. One can move from guilty child to punitive father to needy child and back again in a second, with no real awareness that this process is going on.

What is the way out of this dilemma? What is the passage to some greater degree of freedom? Again, the way out is the process itself. We do not tell people to let it all hang out. We do not tell people to express all their feelings. Obviously, over time we need to learn how to share more of who we are in our relationships. People are very different however, and learning how to share ourselves is very different for each of us. The trick is to develop an awareness that is not part of the transaction that is occurring between two people. Once there is an awareness that is separate, it is not long before the aware ego also begins to separate, and soon there will be some choice as to what happens next.

Both Al and Bea have additional work to do. Bea needs to discover and separate from her primary self and begin to embrace her disowned feeling selves, those that have to do with vulnerability and rage and jealousy. Once she can embrace her power and rationality with one arm, and her emotional selves with the other arm, she can then begin to move into a position where she can initiate a new kind of communication. There is no self that is inherently good or bad; the task is to become aware of and embrace our different selves and learn how to express them through an aware ego. This process is difficult to describe, since it involves tuning into the feeling of what someone says as well as the content.

If Bea were in touch with her vulnerability and did not need to hide it, then her communication to Al might be something like this: "I'm feeling very upset with you and with me. I feel angry and jealous. One part of me would like to kill you and another part feels hurt and another part feels like all of this is nonsense and another part just wants you to hold me. I feel terrible."

Al, too, needs to separate from his primary rational selves and to learn to embrace his disowned feeling selves. If he were able to communicate these, he might say something like: "I certainly do feel attracted to other women, but the truth of the matter is that I love you very much and I need you a lot. Surprisingly enough, there's actually a part of me that feels very guilty about flirting, even though I talk so big and strong about doing my own thing. I sometimes get scared of your anger, and I even am afraid that you might leave me because of it. When I get fearful that way, another part of me gets very angry with you."

Please understand that we are not advocating what one

should do or say. We simply want to point out that when we can separate from our primary selves, we suddenly have many more options available. If we tell Bea that her problem is that she needs to express her anger, then she expresses her anger and this may be very freeing, but if that anger is channelled through the punitive mother in her, it can do more damage than good. We do not know what people should do or say in a particular instance, but we do know that when we can accept these different ways of feeling and being and learn to communicate them with some degree of awareness, relationship becomes much richer and more textured.

The inability to communicate the feelings of the vulnerable child is the primary source of problems and disruptions in personal relationships. Of course, as we pointed out earlier, the answer does not lie in totally identifying with the vulnerable child. People who follow that route become victims in relationship. The key is to be aware of the vulnerability that lies within each of us and to be able to communicate its reality while still being related to the power on the other side. To say to another person: "My feelings have been hurt by what happened this evening and I really am feeling very bad" is not a sign of weakness but rather a sign of empowerment.

Being powerful in relationship means being identified with the parental side and disowning vulnerability. Under these circumstances one learns how to express oneself, how to be very direct about things, and how to get what one wants or needs. It is obviously very important to develop this side of oneself, because if this is not available, it is very easy to be a victim.

Being *empowered*, however, means something entirely different. It means being related both to the vulnerable and the power sides and being able to communicate with both of these selves present. This is an important thing to be learned by all of us who are trying to establish a more conscious system of personal relationships. *Being* in touch *with power allows us to get things done and be successful. Being in touch with vulnerability allows us to be intimate. Being* identified with *power brings authority in the world and a loss of intimacy in relationships. Being identified with vulnerability brings a loss of power and a guaranteed identification with victim status.*

The power and destructiveness of negative bonding patterns are awesome. When they are fully activated, love flies out the window and one's partner or friend can feel like a hated enemy. These are conditions of high stress and pain; some of the deepest moments of human suffering occur during these times. The possibility of verbal escalation into full-scale warfare is very great during these negative bondings. Once a certain point is passed in a bonding interaction, any semblance of awareness disappears and each of us reverts to the law of the jungle.

In thinking about bonding patterns, it is important to keep in mind that, generally speaking, the development of awareness is after the fact and not before. We have to live life and then become aware. If we try to do it the other way, we kill our passions. In a strong bonding pattern, people might yell and scream at each other or become icily silent and cutting and, for us, this is all perfectly natural and inevitable. It is only afterwards that we can begin to examine the interaction to find out what the triggering mechanisms were. This examination will introduce greater consciousness into the relationship, but, despite that, we may be sure that before long another conflict will escalate into war games and we will go through the process again. However, with time, the aware ego begins to enter earlier in the transaction, to have more choice, and to exert a far greater influence over what happens.

Being "Strong" in Relationship

Ed and Clara were at the same party that Bea and Al attended. Ed has also been flirting, though not to the extent of Al in our previous example. Clara is committed to expressing her feelings, and she lets Ed know when they get home that she is angry with him and that she is not going to "take any of this kind of crap" and that "two can play this game as well as one."

Ed has a difficult time standing up for his sexuality. He generally acts in the world as though sexuality does not exist in him except for his marriage partner. He also is very intimidated by Clara's anger. She has had a considerable amount of therapy and has learned how to express her feelings very well. He immediately falls into the guilty/victim son to her attacking mother.

Why might her reactions be called attacking mother rather than just the clearly stated reactions of a woman who is unhappy with her husband's behavior? This is a very important question, and there is no simple answer. Here we must rely on the quality of the reaction. There is a sound, an energy, a vibration, a feeling that one begins to tune into that makes it relatively clear as to what part of the person is expressing the reaction. *One thing to keep in mind is that from the level of awareness and the aware ego, there is no need to dominate and control anyone.* Reactions that come from an aware ego do not have hooks in them. They are not meant to hurt or control people. *Reactions that come from the bonding spaces of the parental voices do just the opposite. They always operate in relationship to a dominance/submission pattern. They always have the effect of controlling the environment.* Invariably one finds that if one person falls into a bonding pattern, the other person is in the complementary pattern. In this situation, if Ed falls into the guilty son, then it is a clear indication that Clara has identified with the negative mother or the revengeful mother.

The ability to react in relationship is very important, something that all of us must eventually learn how to do. As important as it is to learn how to have access to one's emotional reactions, Clara and Ed provide a clear example that it is too simplistic to state as a rule of thumb that one should always express one's emotions. Clara had learned how to express her feelings very well indeed; the problem was that she never learned how to express her vulnerability. Her constant reactions came from a powerful parent within her and they masked the underlying vulnerability that lived in her. *"Being strong" had become her primary self and she had learned how to be powerful. She had not as yet become empowered.* This next step can happen only when her awareness level separates from the power side, and only then does she have the chance to embrace both power and vulnerability. The effect of her reaction on Ed would be totally different under these circumstances and would lead to a totally different kind of discussion between them.

We are describing here a very sophisticated understanding of personal relationship. It is because of these bonding patterns that we find it very difficult to give advice to people about what they should do or say in their personal interactions. There are people who are constantly reacting in their relationships. They share everything and yet their relationships do not work. *The issue is not what is shared but who shares it! What part is giving the reaction?* A reaction that channels through a negative mother will polarize the partner into a frightened, guilty, or rebellious son. A reaction given through a guilty son will activate the negative mother in some form.

Where does it all begin? What self cues off the other self in the partner? It is generally quite difficult to discover how it all begins. It is an interaction that goes on over time, and each of us discovers it at a certain moment. During the course of our own personal relationship, we have tended to stop worrying about causality. Instead, when we become aware of a bonding pattern, we simply take it where it is and examine it as best we can. There is a certain amount of blaming and righteousness that is natural in these bonding patterns. Over time, however, we tend to spend less time blaming, since it only delays separating from the bonding pattern itself. The righteousness that we feel must also be honored, however, as long as it needs to be present. It is a basic companion of the judgmental parent states, so when it is relentlessly present we might just as well accept it and enjoy it.

Love Is Not Enough

It is sometimes awesome to observe the power that characteristic bonding patterns exert over our lives when we are unable to bring some awareness to them and to separate from them. Andrea was married to Antonio, a domineering, South American man who was identified with a macho image of being a man, and who kept her in a the role of a subservient housewife. Her mother, too, had been subservient, and at some point in her marriage, Andrea decided that this was no longer acceptable. So she left Antonio and got herself a job as a home secretary to a very successful older professional woman who happened to be lesbian.

Andrea, a sensual and very attractive woman, soon made herself indispensable to Joan and eventually moved in with her, assuming even more caretaking duties. Before long, they became lovers, with Joan, in her controlling mother self, telling Andrea that she did not believe in monogamous relationships. As the relationship grew in intensity, Andrea's primary self re-emerged to protect her vulnerability. Andrea became the dutiful housewife to Joan's successful businesswoman. The initial phases of the bonding were idyllic. Joan, who had disowned her own housewifely nature, had a home that was beautiful but cold. It was like an extension of her office. She did nothing to take care of or nurture herself. With Andrea there, Joan was cared for as never before in her life. Her house was a home, her clothes were kept in order for her, her car was fixed, there was always good food. Andrea even brought Joan a freshly cooked lunch to the office each day. Her vulnerable child was ecstatic and Joan often remarked, "I've never been so well taken care of in my entire life."

Andrea, in turn, would say, "Nobody has ever known how to care for you. I really know you and I can make you happy. I don't want to work, I don't want fame, I just want to stay home and take care of you." As a result of her overwhelming gratitude, Joan promised Andrea that she would always support her both emotionally and financially.

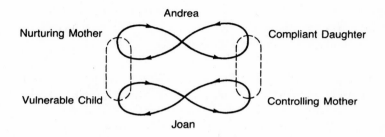

Bonding Pattern of Joan and Andrea

But, as so often happens in these idyllic positive bondings, Joan started to feel stifled and a bit restless, as though she were missing something. In actuality, she was missing something. No matter how loving we are, and Andrea was certainly loving, when we are relating to one another from only a single self, as Andrea was relating to Joan essentially from her nurturing mother, there is something missing—the rest of the person is missing. Joan began to feel stifled by the bonding pattern, but she did not know that she, too, was a part of the dance. All she knew was that she was being smothered and that she needed Andrea to move out of the role of full-time housewife. She encouraged Andrea to spend time outside of the house and to develop new interests. She even encouraged her to have a girlfriend. As we shall see in Chapter Seven, although Joan did not exactly know why she was encouraging this, she was, in essence, trying to break the bonding.

Joan's behavior made Andrea even more vulnerable, so she intensified her efforts to be nurturing. She became intensely jealous of Joan's involvement at the office and of her affairs. She told Joan that she needed her at home more

often so that she could care for her better. Finally, when none
of this worked, Andrea got herself a girlfriend to make Joan
jealous. At first, Joan was relieved; now she was no longer the
sole recipient of Andrea's attention. But when the new
girlfriend started to send Andrea roses every day, Joan
found, much to her surprise, that she was jealous. As she
said, "It just doesn't go with my belief in freedom to be
jealous like this. I'm really surprised."

Despite this jealousy, Joan was not ready to settle down
into a bonded monogamy with Andrea's nurturing, self-
sacrificing mother, as Andrea wished. She continued to push
Andrea to grow beyond the confines of the bonding pattern.
Joan, however, did not learn from the relationship either. She
did not use this as a chance to develop an awareness of her
own fairly extreme denial of vulnerability and her own role in
the bonding pattern. Instead, she continued to disown her
jealousy and possessiveness (although she had fleetingly
admitted these to her therapist), her vulnerability, and her
own nurturing mother. Andrea, in turn, continued to disown her power, her businesswoman, and her independent,
outgoing woman of the world. In a most fascinating turn
of events, Andrea returned to her husband where she
could comfortably resume her role of hurt daughter/self-
sacrificing mother to Antonio's demanding, unappreciative
father/needy son. In this way, she continued to remain fully
identified with her role as the self-sacrificing, nurturing
mother and abused daughter.

Joan, needless to say, was horrified and pointed out that
Andrea was going right back to where she had come from.
Joan never did realize that Andrea had lived the same bonding pattern in their relationship. Andrea had been the hurt
daughter to Joan's controlling mother and the self-sacrificing
mother to Joan's essentially disowned needy daughter.

The Disapproving Mother

Few subpersonalities can strike terror in the heart of a man as well as the disapproving mother when she appears in her most virulent form. One look from her cold, disapproving eyes and the strongest, most self-assured man will crumble. He may well reconstitute quickly and bring forth some power side, but, underneath, his child has been struck down quite effectively. When the disapproving mother makes her appearance, there is a withdrawal of love energy, and in its place is a pitiless judge. This disapproving mother, however, is often present in a much milder form. Basically, in primary relationships, the disapproving mother is to the man what the withdrawn father is to the woman. The withdrawn father can usually turn a woman into a needy daughter while the disapproving mother can usually turn a man into an awkward, bumbling son. Let us see how Laura's disapproving mother, who is of the milder variety, affects Sam.

Laura is a bit of a perfectionist, as were her parents. She likes things done "the right way" and believes in appropriate behavior and good manners. She has raised her children to be ladies and gentlemen, and she is basically disapproving of anyone who is thoughtless, unmannerly or, as she would see it, vulgar. However, Laura is not a total prig. She has begun her own consciousness process and is not fully identified with her perfectionist any longer. She has even developed a sense of humor about her perfectionistic tendencies and her demands for others to also be beyond reproach. But Laura's disapproving mother, although much modified, is not totally out of the picture.

A great deal of Laura's change in consciousness has come about as a result of her marriage to Sam. Sam is more relaxed about these matters. He realizes that nobody is perfect and so he does not have perfectionistic demands upon himself. He appreciates people for who they are and is not particularly impressed with how they behave. He has helped Laura move beyond her concern with the superficial and into a deeper appreciation of the whole person. Now, we must be quite clear about this—Sam is no slob! He, too, has been raised in a family where he was taught manners. In fact, his mother was a bit more like Laura than it might first appear. His mother, too, had a need for Sam to be a gentleman and a credit to her. So, although Sam is not as preoccupied with appearance or manners as Laura, he is usually appropriate in his behavior. Also, since he has been with Laura, he has begun to pay a bit more attention in these areas and his behavior at the table, in particular, is generally quite fine and does not create any problems for anyone.

One day Laura is particularly tired and feeling a bit overwhelmed. She comes home from work, and Sam is not there to greet her and help her prepare dinner as he usually does. He has had to stay late at work to finish off with a client. Laura is feeling particularly vulnerable because of her exhaustion and, as we have seen so often in our bonding patterns, she ignores her vulnerability and pushes herself forward. She fixes dinner and has it ready for Sam when he arrives home. But, by the time Sam arrives home, it is not Laura but a disapproving mother who greets him at the door.

Laura is not aware that her disapproving mother has taken over; she just notices that Sam needs a haircut and that his shoes need shining. (His hair and shoes had looked fine that morning.) As she looks further, she thinks that his trousers could use a pressing and that the shirt is not quite to her taste. She does not say anything, but by now Sam is feeling uncomfortable and he does not know why. He just feels wrong. By the time they sit down at the table, they are in a full energetic bonding pattern.

At the dinner table, a strange thing starts to happen. Sam, who has been feeling a bit uncomfortable, becomes more and more awkward. He seems to have trouble keeping his food on his fork, he spills the sauce on his shirt, he slurps his soup, and he seems to get crumbs on his face with each mouthful. He gets more and more uncomfortable as Laura and her daughter (who, by now, has also become a disapproving mother) watch incredulously. Not a word is spoken. Sam becomes more and more awkward and bumbling and Laura and her daughter become more and more disapproving. The meal continues in silence and discomfort for everyone until Laura finally says, "Could you please stop slurping your soup? I can't stand it." Sam, switching from awkward son to rebellious son, says, "Will you please stop telling me what to do! You two are a real pain at the table. I don't like eating with you" and he leaves the table.

Later that evening, when the intensity of the bonding pattern has lessened, Sam and Laura try to figure out what had happened. They have learned that these patterns can be teachers. They realize, not without amusement, that when Laura's disapproving mother takes over, Sam has no place to move energetically but into the awkward, bumbling son. Although he is perfectly adequate most of the time, when this son takes over, it's good-bye to any semblance of self-confidence, grace, or adequacy. In retrospect, the picture of him at the table dropping food on himself as Laura and her daughter get more and more disapproving is very funny, and they have a good laugh. When this all was actually happening and the bonding pattern was in full force, it was not quite so funny.

The Energetic Reality of Bonding Patterns

The interactions between people in these bonding patterns are not just psychological; they are also energetic. When Laura is in her disapproving mother, Sam's awkward son is literally pulled forth. These bonding patterns are experienced as a very real physical event between two people, even though the people involved may not know what is happening in physical terms. We call this an *energetic linkage*. One of the best examples of this occurs in the interaction between the withdrawn and impersonal father of a man and the daughter side of a woman. Typically, when a man's feelings are hurt, he withdraws into an impersonal father. Usually, the woman goes into a daughter self in response to this withdrawal, feeling quite bereft and trying very hard to get the man to feel again, to respond to her in a more personal way. She can see that he is withdrawn on a psychological level. She may even recognize that his feelings have been hurt and that this is how he handles the situation.

What is generally not known is that there is an actual withdrawal of physical energy on the part of the man. The woman is literally suffering from a loss of physical contact, because a strong energetic interaction is a real warm physical connection. The woman may actually feel a chill or a loss of balance when this interaction is interrupted. It is a decisive shift in the energetic linkage between them. This is one of the reasons why women get thrown as deeply as they do into daughter roles when the man pulls back energetically into the withdrawn father. It is like being in the midst of a delicious dinner and having it suddenly taken away from you.

Women who have been raised in families in which the father has been unavailable emotionally—and this is very common—are familiar with this withdrawn father/victim daughter bonding pattern, and they enter into it quite easily in their relationships. It involves a dreadful, physical feeling of loss and a desperate willingness to do anything whatever to reinstate the previous feelings of well-being. Women who come from families in which this is not the pattern, and in which they are accustomed to being met emotionally and energetically by their fathers, are less likely to fall into this particular bonding pattern but will instead react to the man and help pull him out of his withdrawal.

A wonderful example of the energetic reality of bonding occurred one evening a number of years ago when there were no children at home. We were alone and we were sitting on the couch facing each other, feeling the most wonderful energetic connection between us. Our heart areas felt like vibrating machines, they were buzzing so strongly. Suddenly, Hal became aware of the fact that the buzzing had stopped. It was like an emptiness, like being dropped out of paradise. He asked Sidra what had happened. Sidra told him that she was trying an experiment. She had visualized one of her daughters in her bedroom, while still trying to maintain the contact with Hal. The act of visualizing her daughter had totally broken the energetic connection between us.

This was a remarkable experience for both of us. It helped us to experience the physical reality of the bonding energies and the great power of the energetic connection between Sidra and her children. It helped Hal to understand with absolute clarity that so long as the children were around, this connection would exist. It is perfectly normal and natural and without it, the children would grow up incorrectly. What Hal further realized was that if he wanted to feel Sidra's full energies, then he had to do something to take her out of her home environment. Rather than complain and enter into a bonding pattern because his vulnerability had been triggered, he would have to use his impersonal energies through an aware ego and act. This was a very profound insight for both of us and marked an important shift in our relationship.

Personal and Impersonal Energy: A Bonding Natural

The way that people use personal and impersonal energy is a major contributor to bonding patterns in relationship. We have spoken a bit about this in the last chapter, but now we wish to add further to your knowledge of these particular energy patterns. Let us, first of all, define what we mean by these terms. *Personal energy* refers to a way of being with people that is related, friendly, and warm. Most important, the recipient of personal energy generally experiences a true contact with the other person. When we use personal energy, people feel received by us; they feel personally acknowledged.

Impersonal energy, on the other hand, is objective. It is focused more on ideas than personality. It is less concerned with whether or not a person is being received. With personal energy, we tend to move out toward the other person. With impersonal energy, we hold back more; we are more contained. Impersonal energy might be described as more objectively based and certainly having less to do with feelings. These two contrasting energies create a bonding field-day in relationships. Let us see how this might look.

Maurice and Beth Ann are married. In addition to being very much in love with each other, they are also very different from one another. Maurice is a high school teacher in the physical sciences. Beth Ann is an elementary school teacher. Her friends would describe her as warm, loving, caring, and always available for personal contact. Maurice is not at all personal, does not express his feelings easily, and many of their friends would call him aloof. In the intimacy of their bedroom, Maurice is able to let down and show his more feeling and vulnerable sides to Beth Ann. She is able to bring her more impersonal energy to the work situation in planning her time and taking care of the necessary details, but that is the only place her impersonal energies are available.

One Sunday morning Beth Ann receives a call from a friend who is very upset and in need of help. Being the warm person that she is, her first reaction is to invite her friend over to talk, which she does. This happens quite spontaneously, and as soon as she hangs up the phone, she has a funny feeling. She has not talked to Maurice about it, and she feels guilty because she knows that Maurice likes his privacy, especially on a Sunday. At this moment she enters into a full-blown guilty daughter attack. Such a pattern is guaranteed to bring out the punitive father in the man. She thinks of going to her friend's house. She thinks of cancelling. Within seconds she is totally frazzled, in a full daughter bonding to the withdrawn/impersonal father in Maurice. Interestingly enough, all this is going on inside of Beth Ann. However, Maurice is a part of the bonding pattern, too, even though he knows nothing about what is going on in this particular situation. They have danced this energetic dance many times before.

Let us examine this bonding pattern from Beth Ann's perspective. In her family upbringing, the modeling that she experienced was all personal. The family environment was very loving and caring; few limitations were ever set. Her mother was almost saint-like in her willingness to help people, and her father was passive and accepting. She had two brothers, the older one of whom was quite withdrawn, a bit of a recluse. Beth Ann was the center of the family, the real star. The problem was that she had no experience with impersonal energy. She had no ability to separate herself from the feelings and requirements of another human being, one of the gifts of impersonal energy. She blended with people totally when she was with them, and their feelings and problems and lives became her feelings and problems and lives. The problem was not that she said yes to her friend that Sunday morning. The problem was that *it was not she who said yes!* Her primary selves said yes, and since she was identified with her primary selves, there was no self on the other side that could bring a balance into her life.

Of course, Beth Ann married her disowned self; we all do. What is necessary is that we appreciate why this has happened. We must learn to recognize what it is that we have disowned, so that we can begin the job of embracing that energy and making it a part of our reality. Otherwise our partner remains forever stuck with our projections.

When Maurice finds out what Beth Ann has done, he is very angry. He is not used to showing his anger, and so he withdraws into his favorite place, his impersonal self. Impersonal energy does not have to be experienced as withdrawn. It can be used in a way that is simply an objective, straightforward way of being. However, it is seen in relationships in its withdrawn form with remarkable frequency. Men are particularly expert at this kind of withdrawal, and if a woman has no connection to her own impersonal energy, she is repeatedly forced into a pleasing and guilty daughter. For many men, the identification with the impersonal and withdrawn father is an amazingly effective way to punish naughty wives and turn them into victim daughters. It is also a beautiful way to keep a man away from the reality of his own vulnerability. Beth Ann was in a full daughter identification when she told Maurice about the call, so it would be natural that he would hook right into the father side.

From Maurice's perspective, it is clear that his primary selves are more impersonal and rational. He has disowned the feeling and more intimate selves that are carried by his wife. In his family upbringing, feelings were not safe to express. His control side emerged as a primary self when he was very young, as a way of protecting his vulnerability from a disturbed family environment. To fulfill himself, and the relationship, Maurice must separate his awareness from his primary self and begin to embrace the selves on the other side. Otherwise, Beth Ann must forever carry these parts for him. At yet a deeper level there lies his vulnerability. When he discovers what Beth Ann has done, his inner child feels hurt and abandoned. From the standpoint of the child, the most insignificant appearing incident is experienced as total betrayal, as abandonment. If we are not aware of this, we can see what chaos this unconscious vulnerability can play with our lives.

We can see in this example the remarkable opportunity that relationship gives to us. The very things that exist between couples that cause disturbances and upset and trauma, when looked at from a different vantage point, bring with them the possibility of redemption. Maurice says to Beth Ann: "I can't stand it when you are so weak and when you can't ever say no!" Yet her very inability to set limits, the way she blends, her compassion and feeling, all of these selves are begging for redemption in him. He has not been able to reach them in his personal life before the marriage. Now he has his chance to heal himself, if he can but step back and see Beth Ann as the teacher that she is for him. Relationship as teacher! That is the key over and over again.

It is not enough for Beth Ann to keep falling into the daughter role with Maurice. He is her teacher and when she recognizes this, then she can say to herself: "There is something in Maurice that is missing from me. I must discover in myself the ability to step back as he does, to be less personally involved, as he is. Then I will have more choice in my life as to whether I say yes or no to a friend." One of the things that makes this more difficult to appreciate is the fact that the redemptive energy is seen in its more negative form. Beth Ann's feeling side tells her that she must not be cold and impersonal like Maurice. Unless she understands that the impersonal energy is channeling through the withdrawn father, she will have a difficult time staking her claim to this impersonal energy. We each need an understanding of bonding patterns to be able to appreciate the quality in the other person that is causing the problem for us.

The ability to embrace in ourselves the opposites that are carried by our partners and friends shifts relationship dramatically. There is much less stress, more conscious time with one another, and the development of a much more profound intimacy. The work we do to understand this amazing process of bonding is well rewarded. It can heal old wounds. Relationship itself changes dramatically because there is the excitement of joint exploration that brings an added dimension to the interaction. There is plenty of misery in the world of personal relationship, and particularly primary relationships. It seems clear from our experience, however, that a lot of the misery can be cleared away if people are willing to do the ongoing work necessary to develop consciousness in relationship. It doesn't happen automatically. Let us now continue in our exploration of common bonding patterns in primary relationships.

Money and Who Controls It: Another Natural for Bonding

Money, and how it is used in relationships, is another major focus for bonding patterns. Our cultural conditioning has created certain stereotyped sex roles for men and women in terms of the way money is used in a relationship. Historically, the man was in charge of the finances and the woman took care of the home with the money that he gave her. It was certainly not a partnership. Today things are amazingly complex because of the new role of women in society, because of broken homes and second marriages, and because of the desire of many couples to meet the whole issue of money in a new way. Let us look at a few examples of bonding patterns that are connected to money and the way it is used.

Don and Risa were spending a pleasant Saturday afternoon together strolling around a lovely shopping area near their home. They passed a Porsche dealer and went inside to look at a car with a price tag of over $40,000. They left after a time and went on walking, but Don was hooked, and, after a while, he said to Risa, "Gee, I sure would like to have a Porsche." In the way they relate to money, Don is the spender, or the one who wants to spend, and Risa is the one who is always setting limits. They have created a natural bonding of mother/son in this respect.

We may safely assume that the voice in Don that said "I want a Porsche" was, in fact, his needy son who always wants things. Risa was immediately, as always, thrown into mother. From her standpoint, not only did she always have to set limits, but she also had the humiliation of not having any real voice in how the money was spent because it was his money. This is a very common phenomenon in primary relationship, and, when it exists, it automatically throws the woman into a daughter position, with very deep resentment operating in her at some level.

Risa contracted into her mother self and said from that

self: "Here we go again. We owe over ten thousand dollars on the car we have and now you're talking about buying a Porsche." There was a sting to the voice, for in this mother self, she was on the attack. All of her anger and resentment at not having control of the money was filtering through her reactions. If we were to dig down to her real feelings, we would discover that her real reaction to Don's statement was one of vulnerability and fear. They were short of money for a variety of different reasons and one of these was his profligate spending. She hated feeling the insecurity of financial deficit but could not communicate her feelings of fear and vulnerability. If she could, they would sound something like this: " You know, Don, it really scares me when you say that, even though I know you're not ready to buy the car. I really get frightened about money." These feelings were not available to her, so instead, she slid into a natural mother bonding in reaction to the fear and she became the attacking mother. This is an amazingly frequent pattern in primary relationship.

Don naturally rose to the bait. That is what is so much fun about bonding patterns. They are so deliciously predictable, unless they happen to be your own. Don had started off in the needy son and then he shifted into the more defensive son. He said to her: "Oh I don't know. If we sold our car privately I'll bet we could work out a deal where our payments might be maybe twice what they are now. Besides, it's a good tax writeoff." Risa escalated very quickly and brought in her resentments about the whole way that money was handled between them. She said, with considerable anger: "Just do what you goddam please! It's your money anyhow!"

Don's feelings were, of course, hurt by this, but he was long past knowing this and leapt into the angry and punitive father, telling her that she should mind her own goddam business and that he would do exactly as he wished with his money. War was officially declared, and the full impact of the bonding hit home for both of them. To complete the drama, that night he wanted to make love and that, of course, was the

farthest thing from Risa's mind and body. Negative bondings make us feel bruised and injured and, until we separate
from them, we are not likely to achieve a good sexual
connection. Don went on the offensive but underneath was
his vulnerable child feeling quite abandoned and needy
because Risa had withdrawn from him.

This feeling of neediness on the part of the vulnerable
child, when unconscious, often translates itself into sexual
desire. From Risa's position, sex was unthinkable. Don went
into yet a deeper rage, telling her that she was frigid and that
she should see a psychiatrist, and that he did not know how
much longer he would put up with her "crap." The fact that
they had made love the two previous evenings was quite
beside the point. These negative bondings cause reason to be
thrown out the window. They are very difficult and very
sad, and yet the way out of them is clearly mapped once we
begin to see the nature of the bonding and the disowned
selves that are connected to them.

To step out of the bonding dance and to learn from it
requires several different steps on the part of Don and Risa.
First of all, both need an awareness level that can witness
what is happening. An awareness level could help Don to
witness the rage and vitriolic anger he has fallen into once
again, for it is a pattern that has repeated itself over and over
again in their relationship and in the marriages that had
preceded this one.

Don also needs to begin to see the way that he sets Risa
up in these situations. To do this he would have to become
aware of his manipulative son and his disowned business
person. So long as he disowns his inner business person or
fiscal conservative, Risa has to carry this for him. If he had
his business person available, he wouldn't be seduced by the
Porsche in the first place. He would be able to evaluate the
finances and not make her responsible for his own fiscal
conservative.

Risa, from her side, has no idea of how she constantly
falls into the fiscal conservative and the contracted mother.

The voice in him that is always wanting things consistently hooks into her mother self. From this place she has no connection to her vulnerability and fear as we have pointed out before, and so the interaction between them remains in this bonded state.

Where has love gone? It has disappeared and in its place is grief! The amazing thing is that when the awareness level kicks in and when people begin to catch hold of their disowned selves and see how the other person is carrying them, the feelings of love can be restored. There is no guarantee that a relationship is forever. When people begin to separate from bonding patterns, relationships usually either improve dramatically or they end. However, if the relationship does end, it ends in a very different way because both people have gone through major changes. The ending is a natural part of their developmental sequence.

Every primary relationship needs a psychological divorce. By a psychological divorce, we mean the ability of an aware ego to disengage from the bonding patterns. At one point in our own relationship Hal had the following dream:

> I'm getting a divorce from Sidra. The judge asks me: "Why are you getting a divorce?" I answer him: "Because we're so much in love!"

In relationship, we need love and we need a consciousness process. Both are essential. *Separating from the bonding patterns supports a different kind of love, and that new kind of love, in turn, supports the desire to separate from the bonding patterns.*

The Patriarchal Heritage and Money in Bonding Patterns

Cindy and Ron are a very wealthy couple who have been married for over twenty years. The relationship is one of strong bonding patterns with very little awareness. He controls the money; she is the daughter to his patriarchal father in this and in many other matters. On the other side, she is very much devoted to him and cares for him unstintingly from the mother selves. There is some awareness of these patterns that exist between them, but it is minimal.

Cindy's daughter, Ann, is a strong feminist, and she resents her mother's "daughter" role with her father. The women are out shopping for antiques one day and a very attractive salesman begins to flirt with Cindy. Ann enjoys this immensely. Eventually Cindy finds a beautiful antique that she would like to buy but that costs in the neighborhood of twelve hundred dollars. She feels, however, that she cannot buy this without her husband's permission and authority. Ron, on the other hand, would not hesitate to spend any amount of money on anything he might want, and it would never occur to him to ask Cindy's permission. Ann is very annoyed with her mother because of her passivity and her seeming dependence on Ron.

When they return home, Cindy tells Ron about the antique she wants to buy. Ann, however, tells him about the salesman and how he flirted with her mother. Ron goes into a very impersonal mode and comments in a rather withdrawn manner that, in order to buy the antique, he would have to sell some stock. He insinuates that this is a bad time to do so. This hooks Cindy immediately and she says: "Oh no—you don't have to do that. It really isn't that important!" This settles the purchase of the antique. It does not settle Ann's anger toward her mother and father and what she perceives as his patriarchal dominance.

The good daughter in Cindy is a powerful self and determines a great many of her personal interactions. It is quite easy to see that Ann became an ardent feminist so that she would never become a "good daughter" like her mother. Interestingly enough, both Ann and Cindy are strongly identified with daughter selves. Cindy is identified with the good daughter and Ann is identified with the rebellious daughter. Whether good or rebellious, both are daughters and each role constitutes an imprisonment in that they are both in constant reaction to the father side of Ron.

The bonding patterns in Ron are interesting to explore in this situation. From the beginning of the interaction he was clearly in the father self. His wife was playing the good and pleasing daughter and his real daughter was playing out her rebellion to what she perceived as his patriarchal and dominating nature. She gets back at him when she describes the way the salesman was flirting with her mother. Ann knows at some level he is sensitive to this kind of thing, and the rebellious daughter in her will do anything to bring about his downfall. His response to the situation is that he will have to sell some stocks in order to purchase the antique piece. It is the response of a controlling father and a manipulating son. He has also withdrawn into an impersonal self (which can be a facet of the controlling father). Objectively speaking, what he says is patently ridiculous; he would spend ten thousand dollars on something that he wanted, without batting an eye. In fact, his feelings were hurt and his vulnerability was threatened when he heard about the flirtation. Ron is very cut off from the child within himself, however. When a man's feelings are hurt and when he is not aware that they are hurt, the man goes into the father/power side to balance the equation. The withdrawn father takes over and, underneath it, is a hurt child. Ron's withdrawn father soon becomes controlling father, since this is his general way of dealing with any situation that threatens his vulnerability.

The issue is not whether or not Cindy buys the antique. She has an opportunity in a situation like this to separate from a behavior pattern that has been with her all her life. She was the good and pleasing daughter to her parents, and this was then transferred to her husband. The problem was that she never felt like a real person. How could she, when she lives her life as a daughter to everyone? Interactions like this one with Ron create a golden opportunity for her to become aware of, and to separate from, these patterns, to begin to feel like a responsible and fully functioning adult. The issue is not whether she buys or does not buy. The issue is, who is it that buys or doesn't buy? What self is in the driver's seat?

From Ron's side, an equally important opportunity becomes available. He has always been the responsible father, very much the patriarch and very much cut off from any relationship to his vulnerability. It gets taken care of at an unconscious level by Cindy, but never has he been able to admit his own feelings of weakness, vulnerability, and fear and to make these a part of the relationship. Never has he been able to relax and allow someone else to take the responsibility of caring for him. How different a relationship it would be if his own neediness were conscious and expressed! How different a relationship it would be if he were not always the knower and the one who had the final say in things.

Identification with the Good Parent and Its Consequences

The identification of a man with the good father is a natural entree into a vast array of possible bonding situations. Let us examine a few of them to see how this works.

Dan and Ginny have been dating for about four or five months. They take a holiday trip to another city, and Dan tells Ginny that he wants to buy her a dress as a gift. Ginny is thrilled and they go to a dress shop that she has heard about. Dan is a good father type. He is very giving and is always doing things for people. So long as he is identified with the good father, he cannot say no. He cannot set limits, even when Ginny picks out a dress for five hundred dollars. Because she is very excited about it, Dan buys it for her. Since the good father is his primary self and he is fully identified with this role, he is unable to set any kind of limits as to how much she can spend. It never even occurs to him that he might do so.

Later, after their weekend is over, he is furious with her.

She, however, never learns anything about how he feels, because he breaks the relationship and never expresses any of these angry, exploited feelings to her. He feels that she is selfish and uncaring and that she has no concern for his welfare. If she cared at all about his feelings, he mutters to himself, she would have asked him whether the amount spent was reasonable for him.

Good fathers must have corresponding daughters in their relationships with women. It may be a good daughter or an "I want" daughter. Whatever the case, the father will have his daughter. Because he was so identified with the role of good father, Dan was unable to embrace the other side of himself, which remained a disowned self. The other side would contain the selves that have to do with setting limits, being personally selfish, and being related to his own needs rather than to the needs of other people. If Dan had been in touch with the other selves, he might have established a very different kind of communication with Ginny. He might have said to her: "Ginny, I'd like to buy you a gift of an outfit you really like. You can spend up to three hundred dollars for it." In this way, Ginny would have had some guidelines. Without them she was indeed thrown into her hungry little girl, and the "I want" daughter part of herself took over in the shopping situation. Because she was identified with the daughter who was being taken care of, it could not occur to her to ask him how much he felt comfortable spending.

Dan's feelings were constantly being hurt by other people in this way. He would promise too much or give too much and then, at some point, the negative side of the father would come in and he would feel resentful and judgmental at the way the other person was taking advantage of him. What happens with good fathers and good mothers is that the world outside gets cared for, but the personal needs of the individual are neglected. The inner child is neglected. At his core, Dan's feelings were hurt by the fact that Ginny spent so much money without regard to what he could afford. He could not set limits in the first place, and he could not communicate the hurt feelings in the second place. The result was heavy judgment and anger and the eventual end of the relationship. At no point was he able to see his part in the interaction. He remained righteously angry, and terminating the relationship was the natural thing to do so far as he was concerned. If there is one thing that negative fathers know how to do, it is to be righteous!

The identification with the good father and good mother is one of the most basic patterns that we find in relationship, and one of the strongest contributors to bonding patterns. Let us look at some other examples of how these patterns affect relationships. In our book, *Embracing Our Selves*, we cite the dream of a woman who is very much identified with this good mother/responsible mother self, almost to the exclusion of any other part of her being. Because of the power and clarity of this dream, we are repeating it here. Marilyn, a woman in her thirties when she had this dream, had spent her life identified with the role of mother. The dream occurred at that point in her process when her awareness level was beginning to disengage from this maternal pattern.

> Sounds have become acute. There is so much noise and confusion that I cannot rest. I finally become fully awake, and I look about me. It is as if I were in a strange house, and yet I know that it is my house and that I have lived in it for a long time. There is a mirror across from my bed, and I glance at it. I am horrified to see that I have grown old while I slept. The noise is deafening, and I go out to try to find where it is coming from. As I reach the kitchen door, I realize it comes from there. Around the kitchen table are many people, some young, some older by far than I am. They are all dressed in children's clothes and are waiting to be fed. They see me and begin to pound their bowls on the table and call "mother" to me.
>
> I see my priest across the room with his back to me, and I think that surely he can explain this to me, but as I approach him he turns around and I see that he is wearing a bib and is holding a bowl too! I run back to the door to leave. As I pass the table, I see my parents there, wearing bibs like all the rest. I

reach the door as a man comes in. I know him to be my husband, although he is not the husband I had when I went to sleep. He makes a pass at me and I feel relieved, thinking at least he doesn't think I'm his mother. When I look at him, however, he is wearing knickers and his face is the face of a child. I think that this is a nightmare, and I run and shut myself in my room in order to wake up more fully, but I know I am not asleep. I ask myself over and over again: "What have I done while I slept?" Ray comes into the room (Ray is a therapist in the city where she lived). I think that surely he can help me to understand this, but he is crying because he has hurt his knee and wants me to bandage it.

We said before that to be identified with a particular self, and to have no awareness of this reality, is to live in a prison. In this dream the unconscious provides a different metaphor. It says that Marilyn has been asleep and she only now is beginning to awaken. Being identified with our primary selves is like being asleep. We think we are awake (conscious), but in fact we are asleep, because there is no aware ego that is separate from the primary selves. Awakening comes when we separate from our primary selves and can begin to hold the tension of the opposition that exists between the primary self and whatever is on the other side. In Marilyn's situation, she begins now to become aware of her own personal, more selfish needs. These must be balanced against the part of her that continues to respond as the mother. In a later chapter we will be discussing the dream process and how valuable it can be in supporting and deepening the understanding of our personal relationships.

Good Fathers, Good Mothers, and the Denial of Instinct

It is often the case that the identification with the good father and good mother selves can result in a feeling of fatigue and ennui. There are a number of reasons for this. Taking care of other people all the time and not providing time for one's personal needs begins to get wearing after a while. Personal selfishness means that we do things for ourselves, and when we do things for ourselves we have more energy.

Identification with these patterns has another consequence. Individuals identified with good mother and good father selves are generally disconnected from their instinctual lives. They have a hard time reacting to people with the honesty of their feelings. There is a strong need to please. This denial of personal needs and the further denial of instinctual life means that a major system of energy is lost to the individual. In addition to this, a certain amount of energy is needed to keep the disowned instinctual selves out of one's conscious awareness. In our own relationship (Sidra and Hal), we have learned that the existence of this kind of exhausted feeling is a sure sign that we have locked into these good parent selves. It is at these times in a relationship that a major fight is likely to erupt, seemingly from nowhere, a fight that brings with it inexhaustible amounts of anger and energy. It is often this very anger that breaks into the bonding pattern and lets people know that they have "fallen asleep."

The identification with the good parent and the corresponding continual denial of instinct and selfishness can sometimes lead to physical debilitation and illness. There are powerful forces in our upbringing that move us toward these good mother/good father ties and the concomitant disowning of instinctual energies. Television sitcoms portray remarkable parents being good, kind, compassionate, and understanding. Natural irritability and selfishness are not particularly acceptable in our society. But people in relationship are not always smooth and gentle with one another. If this is seen as a negative, then every time things are not smooth this is seen as a negative interaction. Let us look at another example of how these parental patterns operate in relationship.

It is evening and Harry and Selma have finished dinner. Harry is feeling rather vulnerable and needy. He has been worried about his health, and he has been experiencing some slight symptoms of dizziness that go along with a blood pressure that is moderately elevated. He has been checked very carefully by a number of different specialists, and they all agree that there is nothing seriously wrong with him. As often happens when he is concerned about himself physically, Henry withdraws into himself because he does not want to bother Selma with all this. This desire not to bother or worry Selma is a pattern of the good father aspect of Harry. His tendency is to stuff many of his worries down his own throat out of this good father identification.

On this particular evening, Selma wants to finish some desk work. Harry is very agreeable to this (good fathers are always very agreeable to things!) and he even volunteers to do the dishes. Selma is used to being taken care of in this way, and her thankful loving daughter responds with warmth and kindness. This is the difficult part of catching hold of these positive bonding patterns in relationship; they often feel so good. Things seem to be working so harmoniously and there is such good feeling and affection.

Harry goes upstairs to read. Selma is a good manager, and once she is at her desk she begins to take care of all kinds of things. She falls into the identification with the managing mother. In this way she takes care of Harry. She makes sure that there is enough money and that their investments are in order. Harry manages things very well in his own business, but in the realm of personal finances, Selma is in charge.

The evening passes and Harry begins to feel resentful. Since he has locked into good father already, his options are fairly limited. If he were not identified with the good father, he could simply go downstairs and tell Selma that he wants to spend some time with her. This option is not available to him, however. Instead, his feelings are hurt and he begins to go into a withdrawal. His "poor me" self becomes stronger.

Then, gradually, a change occurs. From the poor me/ hurt child a new part begins to take over, the angry father. He now resents Selma and her never-ending attention to details. Gone is the gratitude, affection, and warmth. A while later, when Selma comes into their bedroom, she is greeted by a sullen and withdrawn father. She immediately drops into a guilt reaction and the verbal attack is launched by the new Harry. "You are really an insensitive tight-ass. Why do you have to spend so goddam much time at that desk of yours? You'd think the world was coming to an end." Is this the same man who two hours before was kind and loving and compassionate? No, it is not the same man. Harry #1 was identified with the good father. Harry #2 was identified with the "poor me" child. Harry #3 is identified with the negative father.

So long as we are unaware of these selves, we are bounced around amongst them as though we were ping pong balls. Each self takes its swing at us and away we go. If Selma is unaware of these selves, then she automatically falls into the selves that complement the selves with which Harry is currently identified. In this situation, she will become the victim daughter to Harry's negative father. Possibly she might shift into a rebellious daughter and get defensive and fight back. Alternatively, she might shift to the attack herself and fall into her own angry mother side. If her awareness is operating, however, and if she has some experience of these selves in herself and in Harry, she might not have to fall into the bonding at all. She might say to Harry: " Look, I don't know what you're angry about but it's obvious that I've hurt your feelings. I'm sorry that it happened and it would be very helpful if you could let me know what happened!"

One can never predict what is going to happen when one of the partners separates from the bonding. In general, it is quite difficult for the other partner to remain locked into the bonding for a long period of time.

When the awareness level separates from an ongoing negative bonded interaction, humor has a chance to enter into the situation. Negative bonding patterns, if anything, are not funny. They are usually experienced as quite deadly. Yet, once awareness is present, the most deadly situation can become marvelously humorous. George and Frieda are driving out one morning to have breakfast. George is in a strong, angry and withdrawn father. He looks like a black cloud. Frieda is not hooked this time. She says to him, with some humor: "You know, it seems to me we can have a miserable day or a fun day. I'd like to have a fun day. How about you?" It is the tone, the energy that lets you know whether such a comment comes from an aware ego or from a pleasing mother or daughter. In this case, it was the aware ego, and it was very difficult for George, try as he might, to remain locked into the withdrawn father.

We must remember that it is never the content of the words that counts. It is the feeling or energy that accompanies them. Words spoken through an aware ego have an enormous, and surprisingly effortless, authority and power. Parent/child states are always involved with issues of power and control. The gift of awareness is that it is not concerned with power or control. Thus, an aware ego does not need to control anyone, nor does it wish to or need to be dominated by anyone. It is non-polarizing. Harry controls his environment by being identified with the good father. His real feelings lie hidden, and the people around him are essentially manipulated by his goodness. The more of our selves that we share through an aware ego, the less we control people because we have no hidden agenda operating. The parental and child sides of ourselves always have agendas operating.

Sacrificing One's Selves
to Make the Relationship Work

Mark and Ben are in love. They are not identified as gay; they just happen to be in a gay relationship. Mark is older and a fairly successful actor in commercials. Ben is younger and has managed only minor parts. He goes from one "cattle call" to another and is usually disappointed in his attempts to break into the field.

As Ben's lack of success becomes more and more pronounced, he gets increasingly jealous of Mark. They fight viciously and make up with equal passion. They really want to be together. Eventually, however, Ben begins to feel too vulnerable and miserable, and so he gives up and takes over as homemaker in the house. He sacrifices his ambitions and his power side (eventually disowning them) and identifies completely with his nurturing mother self. We might note here that it is common for members of either sex to have selves that are of the opposite sex. This is not confined to people who are gay. Mark's inner child loves Ben's nurturing mother and is truly grateful for being so well cared for. Thus, Mark disowns his vulnerability and submissiveness and Ben disowns his power.

Basically, Mark now has all the power in the relationship; he is the dominant father to Ben's submissive son while Ben's nurturing mother cares for his needy son. There are occasional outbursts and then Mark will buy Ben an extravagant gift to atone for having all the power. As a thoughtful (if dominant) father, he also tones down the reports of his successes so as not to hurt Ben or make him jealous. Ben and Mark are fully bonded and extremely careful of one another's feelings.

Ben still occasionally goes out on auditions, and one day he lands a really good part that brings him some fame in the world of commercials. This immediately breaks the positive father/son bonding that has been operating so smoothly. The negative feelings that have been buried or avoided come to the fore and the negative father/son bonding takes over. Mark's dominant father rails at Ben's submissive son and wants him to continue to care for the house. Ben's judgmental father then attacks Mark's guilty son and tells him, "You don't really want me to make it. You just want me all for yourself." Mark and Ben fight all the time and nobody wants to take care of the house.

Here, despite the unpleasantness of the situation, is an opportunity to grow. Each man could own up to his own vulnerability and each could begin to take care of his own inner child rather than require the other to do so. Each could own up to his own need for success and why, at a very deep level, this is important for his feeling of well-being in the world. Each could own up to his own selfish self that really does want to be taken care of completely, or his competitive self that wants to be the bigger star. It would not be pleasant, but each would learn about himself and each would grow.

But this is not what happens. Both men are now fully identified with their power selves; each man wants to be dominant and each wishes the other to care for his inner child by taking over the housework. There is no awareness; neither has used the relationship as a teacher. In this situation, the subpersonalities have taken over and are driving the cars, each completely attached to the outcome of every interaction. The name of this game is power and control.

This time, it is Mark's vulnerability that wins out. He is getting older and he is desperately afraid of losing Ben. Now it is Mark who stays at home and takes care of the house. He gives up his need for success, he sacrifices his craft, he disowns his selfish and instinctual energies, and he becomes the submissive son/nurturing mother to Ben. Ben is now the one to identify with power and disown submissiveness. We see this so often in a bonded relationship. Regardless of the sex of the individuals, both are willing to sacrifice parts of themselves, to disown them completely, allowing the partner to carry the disowned energy, in order to keep the relationship smooth. Although this may well look like a conscious decision, it is most likely, as it was in this instance, a decision made by the primary selves, usually made with great rationality, to protect the inner child.

It is interesting to note that when a decision comes out of the bonding pattern such as this, there is no aware ego, and therefore there is no real intimacy. If there were, Mark might say something like, "You know, there is a part of me that is truly jealous of you. That part liked being the big shot in the relationship and likes to be the star. But there's another part that appreciates all that you've been through and all you've done for me and is really happy for your success. I really love you a lot. Sometimes I'm afraid that now that you're doing well you might leave me and I really don't want that to happen, so I try to think of things to make you happy. There's another part of me that wants you to feel guilty and miserable that you've surpassed me. It's really a lot of turmoil and I don't exactly know what to do. I do know, though, that I want to be with you."

Again, we are not saying what anybody should do. Many such bonded relationships continue quite pleasantly for a lifetime. In addition to this, it is quite possible that Mark would have come to a similar decision if he had not been operating from his submissive son, but from his aware ego. But, as we have said before, it is not the decision itself, but who makes the decision, that is important in terms of one's own individual evolution of consciousness. In the case of Mark and Ben, neither learned from the other; they just traded places in the very same bonding pattern.

Bonding Through Our Judgmental Selves

This world is a world of judgments, and we think it is safe to say that one of the primary ways people hook into bonding patterns is through the judgmental parent that criticizes other people, or through the inner critic that criticizes oneself. The combination created by the teaming up of an outer judgmental parent in one's marital partner and a powerful inner critic within oneself guarantees abject misery! *Judgment comes through the judgmental parent selves. Discernment comes through an aware ego.* It is a task of the first order for each of us to catch hold of the difference between these two selves. By doing so, the power of the aware ego is greatly enhanced and our whole relational system is markedly affected.

The people who get bonded into our judgmental selves

represent the selves that we have disowned. As we have shown previously, one of the ways that we can discover our disowned selves is to ask the question: "Whom do I judge?" The people we judge are direct representations of our disowned selves.

Sara cannot stand powerful women who act in an authoritarian, judgmental, and dominating way. Sara is much more identified with her loving feelings and has a tendency to be at the mercy of a strong inner critic who criticizes her for any deviation from warmth and compassion. We automatically have a series of bonding patterns set up here between Sara and any strong judgmental female that she happens to meet.

Let us say that she meets Sue, a strong, opinionated, and dominating woman. Sara immediately enters into a bonding pattern because her vulnerable child is activated by the judgmental mother in Sue. Since she cannot handle her vulnerability, Sara's own judgmental and rejecting mother takes over. It may never be expressed verbally, but she can feel its judgments inside. The feelings from this side cause her great stress, and the inner child feels correspondingly more vulnerable because it fears retaliation, attack, and abandonment.

In a situation like this, Sara bounces back and forth between vulnerability on the one side and feelings associated with anger and judgment on the other. These kinds of bondings are responsible for a large portion of the stress we feel in relationships in general. Let us add to this an inner critic that says to her: "You shouldn't be feeling angry; you should be handling this situation better; when are you going to grow up?" Sara is now thrown more deeply into the vulnerable victim daughter and feels more and more helpless in relationship to Sue. It is in this way that our disowned selves, in projected form, invariably become our persecutors in life by becoming dominant factors in our bonding patterns, much as Sara's did.

Dean is a strong, effective, and powerful man who is a

physician. Control is essential for him. He places great demands on his nurses, and he has a reputation for having a very heavy turnover in his office. He hates inefficiency, weakness, and vulnerability. By some strange magic, a large number of the nurses he hires seem to have a fair amount of these characteristics. This happens in bonding patterns over and over again. Dean's judgmental, controlling father literally hires its disowned self over and over again. He wonders why it is that so many nurses have such vulnerable feelings and are so incompetent and needy. He remains locked in a powerful bonding pattern, judgmental father to victim daughter, until each nurse quits because she cannot stand the pressure any longer.

In Dean's case, he also has a son who has these characteristics. This is the nature of these patterns. So long as Dean is identified with the controlling and judgmental father, one or more of his children will very likely be thrown into the victim child, another may possibly be thrown into rebellious child, another may possibly identify with the strong parent and develop in that direction. What we want to illustrate here is how powerful these energetic connections and bondings are, how they determine the direction of lives around us, and how much stress they are capable of creating within us.

Sadly enough, we often cannot recognize a bonding pattern until matters have gotten out of hand or exploded, or until the two people are in an abject state of depression. These situations are not fun, but once people develop a better understanding of the concept of bonding, it is surprising how much faster difficult relational issues can be worked through. It requires real work and time to create a conscious relationship. How else, though, can we discover the nature of these patterns that have affected most of our lives since very early childhood? *The gifts of relationship are many. Certainly one of the major gifts is the possibility of becoming aware of, and separating from, patterns of feeling, thought, and behavior that have been with us all our lives. This separation brings with it an absolutely amazing feeling of freedom.*

The Inner Critic and Its Effect on Bonding

The inner critic is the part of each of us that criticizes us and judges us for the way we think, act, and feel. It is a very powerful self in most people and, once again, most people are not aware of its operation. Some people are aware of the fact that they are critical of themselves, but they do not realize that this criticism comes from a real, live person inside themselves.

Initially, in our younger years, the inner critic's function is protective. Our primary selves are telling us the way we should be in the world and the inner critic is criticizing us for not following these instructions. The inner critic is a function of judgmental parents and siblings and of the family in general. It is a function of collective cultural attitudes and patterns. For example, if a woman reads all the fashion magazines and discovers that attractive women weigh 97 pounds, then the inner critic uses this information and criticizes the woman for weighing 110 pounds. It generally teams up with the perfectionist in creating impossible demands. In the case of women, its strength is added to by centuries of patriarchal consciousness that have negated and demeaned women in many areas. With a good inner critic on the inside, nobody needs an enemy on the outside.

Why do we devote this time to the discussion of the inner critic? What does this self have to do with bonding? One of the very significant ways that we bond with people is through their criticism of us. If our actual parents are critical of us, this tends to throw us into an identification with the victim son or daughter. Once this critic is established inside of us, any outside criticism is reinforced by its inner criticism—not that it usually needs any help. Let us see how this works.

Nanda has been raised by parents who were both very loving and, at the same time, very demanding and perfectionistic. They never told her directly that she was no good or at fault. If she came home with "Bs" on her report card, then the question was why weren't they "As." If she got an "A," the question was whether she had done better than her friends. Nothing was ever quite good enough. In this fecund earth, her inner critic flourished. She married a man who was strongly identified with the judgmental father. Their basic bonding pattern was judgmental father/ victim daughter and guilty daughter. She could never do anything quite right. His criticisms were not always angry or even very overt. The father side needed to dominate her and dominate it did.

What is very important for us to realize, however, is that the bonding pattern between them was maintained with great power by the inner critic in herself that was constantly operating in such a way as to undermine her and support the judgmental father in her husband. They were allies in their need to keep Nanda down, to keep her a victim daughter. If Nanda had been separated from her inner critic, her husband's criticisms would have had far less power. She might even have found his comments funny.

Years later, Nanda came into our program for therapy and training. During a Voice Dialogue session, the facilitator was talking to Nanda's inner critic. What follows is an excerpt from that conversation.

FACILITATOR: You seem like a very powerful voice in Nanda. Have you always been this strong?

CRITIC: Oh, I've been very strong since she was a little girl. I had good teachers. Her parents were fantastic.

FACILITATOR: What about during her marriage? Did you operate then?

CRITIC: Well, during her marriage I was always behind the scenes, but I didn't really have to work too hard. Her husband was so critical that it made my job easy. Actually, now that she's separated from him I have to work much harder than I did before. He's not around, so it's all up to me.

This little vignette is a beautiful portrayal of how the inner critic operates and how much power it has. Without any awareness of this critic, we are always trying to deal with the judgmental parents of the world as a strictly outer phenomenon. Once Nanda could catch hold of this critic, she was simply unavailable for bonding with the judgmental fathers of the world, of whom there are multitudes, just waiting to find their appropriate victim sons and daughters.

Cynthia was a strong feminist. She was in her early twenties and had gone through some very negative experiences with men. She saw men as victimizing women and being totally anti-feminine. She built up a strong emotional charge around this issue. The problem was that she was pulling these negative kinds of experiences into her orbit, and she was finding herself the victim daughter over and over again. She would move from victim daughter to rebellious daughter and then to the attacking mother within seconds of each other.

What finally began to shift things for Cynthia was when, during a Voice Dialogue session, the facilitator talked to her inner patriarch. Here was a voice that boomed from inside herself and spoke about how much he disliked women, how inferior they were, how he wished she were a man instead of a woman, and on and on.

Now this voice within her was conditioned by a patriarchal culture. Fighting this voice only on the outside was like being in a boxing ring with eyes blindfolded and one arm and leg immobile. It is not a fair fight. Cynthia was trying to deal with men on the outside while a major male energy within her was choking her to death. This inner patriarch is one of the forms of the inner critic. When a woman becomes aware of this, she takes a major step out of the victim daughter bonding to the world of the patriarchy.

The inner critic throws each person into the son or daughter role. It is one of the main ways that we bond from these places. If we believe the inner critic, then we are not okay and the person we are with is always right; thus, we automatically enter into a son or daughter relationship with that person.

Neil is constantly criticized by his wife for not being aggressive and forceful enough in his law firm. His wife is not simply upwardly mobile; her ambitions are propelled by a rocket. Neil's father had a very driving personality, and Neil was accustomed to this kind of criticism. He had lived with it since he was a little boy, with a brief period of independence in his dating years. As happens so typically, Neil married his inner critic. He will remain the victim son to the critical mother until he learns to deal with her differently and/or until he learns to recognize the reality and power of the inner critic within himself. It is as if he has been hit on the head by outer and inner criticism for so many years that now it has become a way of life. It feels normal. When his wife goes into her critical mother, he naturally goes into the role of good-natured son. In this way, he remains bonded in a son/mother pattern until he is able to separate from his primary selves.

The tragedy for his wife is that her own judgmental mother is out of control. It has taken her over and at some level she hates herself for it. So long as he remains identified with the victim son, Neil does not have the instinctual power to stop her power mother. In bonding patterns, each member of the team needs the other person for his or her own redemption. It is as though they are in a state of enchantment, held prisoner by their primary selves. If they could use their relationship as a teacher, then Neil would see that his wife carries the power energy that he disowns, he would begin to separate from her power-driven critical pusher and embrace her disowned good-natured self. They would most likely feel much better not only about themselves but about one another.

It is fascinating to think that in our relationships, we have the ability to redeem one another in this way, to help one another separate from the primary selves that have exercised total power in our lives, and to free the disowned or unconscious selves that have not been available to us in the past. Let us continue in our exploration of bonding patterns so that you will see more examples of how this can work.

5

More about Bonding Patterns

Further Exploration of Bonding Patterns

In our last chapter, we discussed the general issue of bonding patterns in primary relationship. In this chapter we will be continuing our discussion, with special emphasis on the role of primary and disowned selves. We will see how bonding patterns operate in family systems and how our disowned selves make us available to bonding patterns in a variety of other relationships. We will also include a brief discussion of transference as a specific type of bonding pattern. First, however, we would like to review some general principles in the consideration of bonding patterns.

It is very important that we treat bonding patterns as normal and natural phenomena. *Bonding patterns are not indicative of pathology. They are operating in all relationships all the time.* They often create powerful feelings of intimacy and closeness between people. The disowned selves provide the keys to understanding the bonding patterns.

Many couples spend their lives in relationships that are quite totally parent/child in nature and there is very little personal growth over an entire lifetime. Yet they lead good and happy lives without any concern about personal development. Each carries the other's disowned selves with comfort, and the bonding pattern does not become overtly negative.

For ever increasing numbers of people, however, this form of relationship no longer works. One of the reasons that so many marriages fail is that the comfort and the concomitant psychological constriction of positive bonding patterns creates boredom and, as time passes, this constriction works to destroy the dynamic life of a marriage.

For people who become concerned with life in a new way, for people who become involved with issues of change and growth, a new kind of relationship is necessary. Once this happens, the understanding of issues of bonding becomes essential. It becomes apparent that when one takes the discomforts of personal relationship as an opportunity for personal growth, the difficulties themselves become an opportunity for a new kind of process, one we might call mutual self-exploration or the mutual evolution of consciousness.

In the last chapter, our considerations applied to all relationships, whether they were male/male, female/female, or female/male. Now we begin to examine bonding patterns in families with children. We do not consider this a comprehensive treatise on family bondings. Rather, we wish simply to give you a feeling of how the bonding patterns in couples are affected by their families of origin, by the addition of children, and, also, to illustrate some of the kinds of bonding patterns that develop between children and parents.

The perpetuation of bonding patterns across generations is a fascinating study in its own right. *One re-creates one's childhood bonding patterns repeatedly until, with the expansion of one's awareness, there is some possibility of choice entering into the system and the opportunity to use the bonding experiences to heal past wounds and to guide one in one's own growth process.* This is illustrated by the bonding pattern of Marilyn and Jack.

Perpetuation of Family Bonding Patterns

Marilyn and Jack have been married for 15 years. Patterns of relating that they do not understand and feel helpless to change have developed in their relationship. Jack is constantly leaving his things lying around the house. He leaves his shoes and socks by the bed, his shirts and pants on the chair by the bed, his underwear on the bed, even though the bag for the dirty clothes is only a few feet away. Marilyn dutifully picks up after him, sometimes complaining and sometimes not. When she complains, his response is: "Aw honey!" She is usually quiet after that.

Marilyn was raised in a family where she took on a mother role early in her life, because her own mother, an anxious woman, focused on her work and was not very nourishing as a mother. Because of this, being vulnerable was not safe in Marilyn's family, so Marilyn disowned her vulnerability completely. Marilyn found that by becoming the mother, her own inner child was made safe. Let us see what this looks like in diagrammatic form.

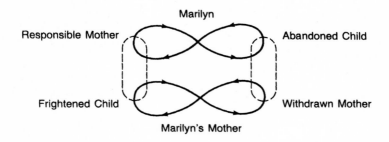

Bonding Pattern of Marilyn and Her Mother

We see in this diagram a beautiful example of the universality of bonding patterns. Here we have a four-year-old child who has become the mother to the child side of her own frightened mother. In this way, Marilyn had protected herself and her own vulnerability because she recognized at some level that the family system was not safe for her. Becoming mother made things safer, and so this became her primary self system as she grew up and entered adulthood.

Marilyn also became mother to her brother and sister, and surrogate wife and mother to her father. Her role in the family became more and more defined by her mother role. It is no wonder that she could move so easily into the mother role in her marriage.

The problem, of course, is that a woman who is identified with her mother self may have a difficult time relating to the world in other ways. Marilyn watches her friends who work and go to school, and she feels envious. As time passes, she feels increasingly resigned to her lot. She becomes more irritable and she does not understand what is happening. She does not feel very sexual toward her husband, which saddens her because at one time the sexual relationship was very powerful and something that they both took very seriously.

Jack came from a family where his needs were met by a very over-indulgent mother. He had a younger sister, but he was clearly the one who was favored by the mother, and his every whim was satisfied. The father was a hard worker and took second place to the mother in every situation. Sometimes Jack would complain and joke about the way his mother doted on him, but he remained very much identified with this pattern. In the relationship to his mother, Jack remained identified with the son self that was constantly being catered to by the mother self of the real mother. Thus, he brought this pattern of relating into the marriage, and almost immediately there was established between Marilyn and Jack a powerful mother/son bonding pattern.

The other side of the bonding pattern is always present, and Jack and Marilyn play this out in their own way. Jack holds a good position and is very responsible so far as earning money and taking care of his family are concerned. At this level, his responsible father self is bonded to the daughter side of Marilyn. He takes care of her. *Her disowned selves have to do with career, work, aggression, and self-aggrandizement. His disowned selves have to do with taking care of himself, order in the home, and time for personal relationships.* He likes to do things that keep him busy; he has no real feeling for just sitting and talking with Marilyn. His relational side is very undeveloped.

The role of children in this kind of relationship is to push both parents more deeply into stereotypical parental selves. Marilyn becomes more identified with the mother role as time passes, and Jack becomes more and more the traditional father. Being busy with children makes it easier to avoid the underlying unhappiness of the relationship. As a full-time mother to her children, husband, dog, cat, and friends, Marilyn's life increasingly feels like a prison. It is not pleasant to think of life as a prison, but fully bonded relationships are just that—prisons with invisible bars, holding inmates who may not even be aware of the fact that they are indeed imprisoned. It is this kind of bonding pattern that can create the fertile earth for affairs, illnesses, physical and emotional symptoms, and oftentimes serious problems that manifest in one or more children in the family.

After 15 years of marriage, Marilyn and Jack have a thoroughly unhappy relationship, though Marilyn is more aware of how unhappy she is than is Jack. They do not scream at each other; rather, they maintain a deadened existence, becoming more and more like strangers living in the same house. The sexuality in the relationship is dead; the vitality is gone. Marilyn feels like a poorly paid maid and is as resentful of her children as she is of her husband. If you asked her, she would say that she loves her husband, though she is not quite sure of what this means anymore.

As we have seen, bonding patterns are operating at all times, with or without conflict. However, conflict situations let us know that the positive bonding patterns have turned negative. Once you begin to examine the basis for the negative bonding patterns, you will start to understand these processes and learn how to work with them. Relationships then have the chance to change in very dramatic ways.

What is it that Marilyn needs to learn? From as early as she can remember in her life, mothering has been her primary path in relationship. Part of her mothering has to do with pleasing people; this way of being in the world has represented the essence of her operating ego. It is her way of protecting that very little girl, or inner child, who lives inside her. That inner child has never felt safe because Marilyn's own parents did not know how to provide proper parenting. (Her family of origin might even be considered dysfunctional.) The primary fuel for Marilyn's anger, bitterness, and hopelessness is this disowned inner child who carries Marilyn's vulnerability. The needs of this child are never met. No one knows about the needy little girl who lives inside her, not even Marilyn. When Tom leaves his clothes all over, her child feels abandoned; she feels unsafe. No one is ever there to take care of her. To avoid the pain she feels, as has always been the case, Marilyn slips into her mother self, resumes her role of caring for others, and the pain of the inner child is gone. This is one of the fundamental dynamics that we find over and over again in women.

Once Marilyn is able to separate from her mother role, then she has the beginning of an aware ego that can appreciate what lies on the other side. Her best girlfriend is an independent, professional woman who has never been married and has never lived any kind of real family life. How often our best friends are direct expressions of our disowned selves! Once Marilyn's aware ego is born, she can begin to become aware of, and to embrace, the parts of her that have to do with work, adventure, romance, and sexuality. She can begin to get acquainted with those parts of her that want to be independent and non-responsible.

Jack, on his side, would have to disengage from the part of himself that slides so easily into the role of the son who needs to be taken care of, a role that he has worn like an old shoe since childhood. If Jack can develop an aware ego that can begin to recognize, and separate from, his own needy child self and start to take care of it on his own, then Marilyn will no longer have to be responsible for it. If she can separate from this mother role to some extent, then she can be freed to be more of a woman in the relationship. Becoming aware of these selves and how they interact with one's partner is the key to developing a more conscious relationship.

In discussing these relationship patterns, we do not give "how to" answers, primarily because there are no "how to" answers. Our aim is to help you develop an awareness of a wide range of bonding patterns so that you will begin to recognize the feelings of these different selves when they come up in your relationships. With awareness comes an increasing ability to deal with friends and partners.

Our Children and Our Disowned Selves

In family situations, it is common for one or more children to live out the disowned selves of the parents. This is because the disowning of a system of energies or selves in a family actually creates an energetic vacuum. Since nature abhors a vacuum, there is a need to fill this space and, all too often, the children do so.

This may happen in dramatic or subtle ways. From the prodigal son of biblical days onward, there have been black sheep in families who pride themselves on living righteous and moral lives. The generous, self-effacing mother is likely to raise tyrannical children who live out her personal selfishness. The driven father is likely to produce at least one ne'er-do-well son.

The existence of the disowned self in one's children creates extremely intense bonding patterns between the parents and these particular children. The righteous father must have his prodigal son reform; the selfless mother is constantly worried about her thoughtless, selfish children; the high-achieving father is deeply disturbed by the son who does not earn his keep. These bonding patterns lock them into one another with great passion. Again, this provides a great opportunity to learn. As usual, relationship presents us with what it is that we have excluded from our lives and gives us the chance to embrace our disowned selves.

Bernie was a successful businessman who disowned his vulnerability, his free spirit self, his playful child, and many other parts that were the opposite side of this business identification. His son lived out Bernie's disowned selves. He hated the business world. He smoked dope and was interested in issues of growth and consciousness. Bernie, in his identification with the responsible and judgmental father, judged his son very harshly, but at the same time, he suffered a great deal of pain at their estrangement.

Bernie was lucky, however. He had a heart attack and he took it seriously. He learned something from it. He separated to some extent from his responsible father role. The judgmental father gradually disappeared and, as it did so, his son moved little by little into the orbit of the business world and eventually joined Bernie's organization.

This is a very common kind of pattern in father-son interactions. Let us examine it in the light of vulnerability as the ignition system and the disowned selves as the fuel for the continuing negative interactions. The inner child was certainly a disowned self for Bernie. Early in his life power became the way to protect his child. His responsible and power selves increasingly negated his fun-loving, free-spirited, sensitive nature. It is very common that when we need to keep things down in ourselves, we also need to subdue them in our children. As Bernie's son showed the characteristics of his own disowned selves, Bernie had to criticize him more and more. Every time he saw his son being overly sensitive, being passive rather than active, or having a great deal of fun, these qualities were triggered in him. Bernie had to stop these tendencies in himself, and the way he stopped them was to attempt to kill them in his son. The things we criticize most in our children are reflections of our own disowned selves.

What happened to change all this? Bernie's heart attack

made him vulnerable. It opened him to the realm of the inner child for the first time. He couldn't be busy, so he had to "be." He began to experience all the previously disowned selves that were an anathema to his primary selves. He learned to listen to his inner child. He learned the importance of play. A new world opened to him and as this world opened, his son was able to move closer to him. He was no longer being polarized to live out the disowned selves of his father, Bernie. They could now learn from one another. Their differences became a source of creativity. They became guides for one another in unfamiliar territory.

Let us now turn to a fairly common mother/daughter bonding. Thelma is a good and responsible and loving mother. She disowns her own selfishness and exploitive nature. Her daughter Terry is, quite naturally, selfish, exploitive, and in every respect her exact opposite. She carries her mother's disowned selves. From a very early age Thelma was bonded to Terry as judgmental mother to Terry's rebellious, selfish daughter. Both were pushed ever more deeply into these opposing selves, a classic pattern in many parent/child relationships. Was Terry inherently selfish? This was not at all the case.

We must keep in mind always that the primary selves develop to protect the vulnerability. Thelma, in her growing up process, learned to become a responsible, good child because this is what worked and kept her safe and rewarded in her family of origin. From a very early age she had been criticized for showing any sign of selfish behavior. This punitive attitude toward selfishness becomes part of her primary self system. When she meets it in her daughter, her primary self system activates because she feels vulnerable and unsafe with any appearance of selfishness. Thus, Thelma becomes "gooder and gooder" as Terry identifies more and more with the disowned self system of the mother until selfishness and exploitive behavior become her primary selves. She may thus become identified with selfishness in her dealings with everyone in her life, or it may simply be with her parents.

The way out of this pattern can be taken by either side, or as happened in this instance, by both at the same time in a therapy situation. Each had to see the other as the teacher that she was. Thelma separated her awareness from her good and loving mother self and began to embrace those selves that were on the other side. She had to find out about the part in her that was not loving, that wanted things selfishly, that resented people and did not want to behave like an angel. Also, Thelma had never learned how to communicate vulnerability with awareness. Instead, she had been identified with her vulnerability and often felt like a victim in life. There is a great deal of difference between communicating vulnerability with an aware ego, and becoming identified with it and thus becoming a victim to others. When this would happen with her daughter, Terry's power side would manifest in very cruel ways, totally out of control, until her mother was the complete victim and felt badly mauled. This of course would make Terry feel more guilty and vulnerable, feelings that she disowned and that she handled by withdrawal.

For her own developmental process, Terry learned how to embrace the loving side of her own nature. She had to learn to separate her awareness from the acting out and rebellious pattern that had marked her life for so many years. She also had to learn about her own vulnerability and how totally she had disowned it in her life. This had the effect of creating a harder and harder exterior. It is so often the case that the parent/child relationships that carry the greatest tension and stress are capable of bringing out the deepest level of personal growth once the nature of the bonding pattern is understood.

Let us look at another of these stress-filled mother/ daughter bondings. Carla is a woman who has been very much identified with her perfectionist. As such, she has always done the right thing. She has completely disowned anything about herself that could possibly be thought of as improper. Her perfectionist self teams up with a very rational self that explains and justifies everything that she does. She has never done anything wrong, she will tell you happily. She has been a proper daughter to her parents, wife to her husband, and mother to her two sons and daughter. From the time her oldest son and daughter entered adolescence, they began to act out in fairly delinquent ways, until their behavior became the source of great heartache to her. She describes her children as the bane of her existence.

Interestingly enough, these familial banes of our existence are direct representations of the disowned selves that lie buried in the shadows of our own psyches. Carla has disowned any part of herself that has anything remotely to do with negative or acting-out behavior. Bonding patterns behave, once they are understood, with mathematical precision.

We would expect one or more of Carla's children to push off of her and identify with a primary self system that is more Dionysian. The excessive use of drugs would be a natural concomitant of this kind of Dionysian identification. Carla's children are in real danger because their acting-out behavior could easily get them into serious trouble with the law. They are the identified family victims. Carla herself is the product of a training in her early life that precluded any hint of the imperfect, any expression of negativity.

We are all products of this natural process of identifying with certain selves or disowning certain selves, until we are able to step out of the magic circle and begin to view our bonding patterns with some degree of awareness. These parent and child interactions are, of course, even more complicated than has been indicated because there are generally at least two parents involved as well as the system of interactions between the siblings themselves. However, there is much that can be learned quickly and easily by getting to the heart of the major bonding patterns and discovering the familiar disowned selves.

Sibling Opposites

One typically finds that when there are siblings, one sibling is identified with one self, or system of selves, and another is identified with an opposite value structure. It almost appears as though there is an unspoken agreement that each sibling stakes out his or her own personal territory. As the years pass these differences tend to harden; the two siblings are thrown more and more into the identification with their primary selves and the disowned parts become much more strongly disowned.

For instance, Ralph is an aggressive, successful older sibling. He has a dominating personality, knows what he wants, and gets it. He is a leader type and brings much credit to both parents.

Larry is a dreamer. He loves music and art, has no clear idea of what he wants, spends much time alone, and, in general, is the total opposite of Ralph.

Ralph is psychologically supported by both parents. They are both rather ordinary in their achievements and they see in Ralph their dream come true. They love Larry, but they see him as weaker. Ralph's achievements make him the special son to the parents, the responsible father to the parents, and eventually the judgmental father to Larry. He becomes more the father to Larry than his real father.

Larry goes more and more into his fantasy, into a world of art and music, disowning with ever-increasing ardor the parts of himself that want worldly success, recognition, and power. Ralph dives ever more strongly into the identification with worldly success and power, disowning with ever more fervor the selves in him that yearn for an opportunity to live a slower, more artistic kind of life. This kind of pushing off from one another represents a fairly typical and classical situation in families.

At some point in our lives, almost all of us are identified with primary selves that are pushing off from the primary selves (our disowned selves) of someone else.

It is fascinating to look at a family and see how the self systems have been divided up. This, by the way, creates intense bonding patterns among siblings; their vulnerability is initially cued off by competition for the love of their parents, and the bondings are subsequently fueled by the disowned selves that they represent for one another. There is usually a responsible sibling who identifies with responsible parent and guilty child, and an opposite sibling who identifies with the dependent child and demanding parent. We frequently see families in which one child is neat and another untidy. (Funnily enough, when these siblings move out of the parental home, the neat one may well become more relaxed and the untidy one, neater.) One sibling devotes time to personal appearance and is the attractive one; the other is the plain one, the intellect or the athlete, or even the wallflower. One is shy and cannot speak about feelings; the other is outgoing and extremely outspoken. One is competent; another is incompetent and disorganized. There is much that these siblings can learn from one another as they break out of the bonding patterns that keep them in their primary selves and that force them to continue disowning the selves that have been attributed to the other.

The Child As Parent

As we have seen, sometimes children identify with parental roles early in their lives and literally grow up as responsible parents. They take care of the emotional needs of their mothers and/or fathers. They become parents to their siblings. When they grow up and marry they naturally have a strong identification with the role of responsible mother or responsible father, and, in this role, they bond into the needy child in their partners and their children. They have learned to disown their own vulnerability and neediness out of a despair that there would never be anybody in the world who would know how to care for them adequately. They do not know how to trust that others will come through for them.

This is a very common pattern in the children of alcoholic or otherwise dysfunctional parents. They look great on the outside, they know how to handle the world through their primary selves as responsible parents, but they feel empty inside because of the disowning of their own vulnerable children. They relate only through the parental bonding pattern and cannot make intimate contact with others until there is a reintegration of the vulnerable child, bringing with it the ability to relate to others.

Nancy was the daughter of alcoholic parents. Her mother had managed to keep things together fairly well until the arrival of her fourth child when Nancy was five years old. At this point, Nancy's mother was overwhelmed and could no longer take care of any of the children. She disowned her own competent mother self and became a needy child. At age five, therefore, Nancy developed what she later called her "five-year-old" mother who, despite feeling woefully inadequate to the task, took over running the household. Nancy had to disown her own vulnerable child because there was no mother to care for it any longer, and she became fully identified with this five-year-old mother. As such, she bonded in as mother to the inadequate side of her real mother. She lived her life in this way, caring for her parents, for her siblings, and, much later, for her clients.

When we met Nancy, she was still identified with this mother part of herself and still taking care of everyone around her with great fear of doing things wrong and constant feelings of being overwhelmed. To everyone on the outside, she was a good and competent mother, but on the inside, she was still the five-year-old trying to act grown-up.

However, as Nancy began to reclaim her own vulnerable child and to explore other parts of herself such as her anger, her resentment, and the part of her that was despairing and did not trust anyone, she began to operate more from an aware ego. She was able to care for others as an adult, from an aware ego, rather than by bonding into them and caring for them as a precocious five-year-old mother. From her aware ego she had a choice as to just what kind of caring seemed appropriate in a given situation. She also had a choice about allowing real intimacy, because she had finally reclaimed her own vulnerability that had been buried so many years earlier.

The identification with the strong father self is quite universal, but it is particularly strong where children have to attend boarding schools at young ages. Ralph is English and was dropped into boarding school when he was six years of age. He literally felt dropped because he had no warning and, what was worse, did not see his parents for six months after they left him at school. This is a very common occurrence in England and other countries where a boarding school education is quite common. Through his whole primary and secondary school education, he saw his parents at most twice a year, sometimes only once a year. He had to become strong. The boys would have laughed at him for crying and being vulnerable, and the teachers were not much different. It was a matter of survival. The boarding school itself became the strong father that totally negated any show of vulnerability. To be vulnerable was to be killed by one's fellow students and/or the faculty. To survive, one identified with the power side, and so it was that Ralph increasingly identified with the strong and responsible father. To shift from this kind of identification into the intimacy of a primary relationship is a rather major step, particularly for people who have had to become strong early in life. The disowning of vulnerability, as we have said before, makes intimacy in relationship an impossibility. A couple may have many things going for them, but with vulnerability absent, something deep and vital and alive is always missing.

Since Ralph spent his youth in the kind of boarding school environment that we have described above, he became aggressive, a powerful leader, and his vulnerability disappeared from view. He grew up into a strong father type, became successful in business, and ultimately married Marti and started a family. Marti had, until now, been successful in her own career, but, as their family developed, she took on more and more family responsibilitjes, grew less forceful with Ralph, and more protective of the children. The oldest child was a boy, Jonathan, and Ralph became an increasingly hard taskmaster when it came to dealing with his son. Jonathan was quite vulnerable as a youngster and Ralph could not bear to see this. Since vulnerability was a disowned self in him, he needed to stifle it in Jonathan. As Ralph became more severe as a father, Marti tried to balance things by being more permissive and giving and loving as a mother. Conflict emerged between Ralph and Marti over their different views about how to handle Jonathan. He began doing badly in school and soon this shifted into an acting-out behavior pattern.

As things got more out of control, Ralph moved more into his primary self of the powerful and demanding father while Marti slipped more into what had become her primary self—the loving and indulgent mother. Jonathan was now the focal point for all of their conflict. Ralph felt less and less understood and more and more isolated in the family. He was increasingly the "heavy," the rejecting one, and everyone was feeling afraid of him. He was quite isolated. His disowned vulnerable child was hurt more and more as the situation intensified, throwing him ever more powerfully into his strong father. It was not until Jonathan's behavior had reached fairly serious proportions that they sought help.

We can see how the problems that Jonathan was experiencing were the symptoms of a family that was strongly bonded with no awareness of what these patterns were about. Our focus of concentration here is on Ralph. Strong fathers are very often the "heavies" in families because of the increasingly severe disciplinary and teaching function they maintain. So long as the aware ego is identified with this strong father self, there is no relationship to vulnerability. There is no relationship to a number of Ralph's other parts, but we are focusing now on the vulnerability. His vulnerability had to be killed in order for him to survive as a child. His power side needed to maintain control and continue to kill vulnerability. Whenever he saw vulnerability in another human being, he went for the jugular. He attacked, he judged, and he criticized. This is how the power side of us maintains its control over our disowned vulnerability.

Every time Ralph looks at Jonathan he feels sick because it brings up so much pain in him. It is the pain that is intolerable and so it is that he must crush the vulnerability out of Jonathan. Thus, his strong father is bonded to Jonathan's vulnerable son, while his own disowned vulnerable son lives more and more in isolation until it hooks in somewhere to have its needs met. This may be an affair, a secretary or some employee or colleague at work, or in friendship that fills the needs of the vulnerable child. The wife in this kind of situation is torn between her love and feeling of responsibility toward her husband and her son, and this can cause an excruciatingly painful situation.

However, if this situation is used as a teacher, if Ralph begins to look to his own disowned child, he could finally begin to heal it, to care for it from an aware ego, and to obtain for it the nurturing it has longed for these many years.

The Child as Surrogate Spouse

As we have indicated, it is a common pattern in family dynamics for one or more of the children to hook into a parent in a strong bonding pattern and become a kind of surrogate spouse to the mother or father. Suzanne provides a good example of this type of bonding pattern.

Suzanne has three children. Ted, the eldest of the three, is her favorite. Teddy is always there for her when she needs him, which now happens with increasing frequency. Her husband, who disowns his vulnerability and neediness, leads a busy professional life, and rather than deal with her ever-increasing sense of loneliness and isolation, Suzanne turns to Ted for her emotional support.

This pattern alienates her husband from Ted, and so Ted becomes doubly trapped. With his mother, he has a strong bonding as good father to her needy daughter and as dependent son to her nurturing mother. As the marital alienation increases, the bonding becomes more intense. With his father, Ted has another kind of bonding. The father becomes increasingly the judgmental father to Ted's vulnerable child.

At a very deep level, the father is profoundly hurt by this "marriage" between his son and his wife. He is not consciously aware of his hurt; he only feels cold rage when he sees them together. His own emotional needs have long since ceased to be met by the marriage, but he also is unable to deal with his wife, to open up the issues that must be addressed to free Ted from the trap he is in.

When we feel empty, someone has to fill the void. Ted and his mother fill this void for one another. Suzanne's husband may have someone else who fills this void for him outside of the marriage, or he may fill it with relationships to his clients in his professional life.

These kinds of bondings to children are difficult for the child, and the most unpredictable things can happen. Ultimately, Suzanne and her husband ended the marriage. Her connection to Ted deepened during the trauma of the breakup and for the following year.

This connection continued until Suzanne met a man with whom she fell in love. He was quite uncomfortable with what he perceived as a mother/son tie that was too extreme. It is exactly in this situation that we get the wicked stepmothers and stepfathers of the fairy tales. Suzanne married this man, and suddenly Ted had nothing. The new stepfather did everything he could to destroy the bond between mother and son. The mother surrendered to the dictates of her new husband because she felt too insecure to make it on her own. Ted was left isolated and quite bereft with no real connection anywhere. He felt totally betrayed as the intense positive bonding to his mother was broken.

The development of behavioral symptoms in Ted ultimately led to a therapeutic intervention in which all of the
family members began to examine their roles in what had
happened. Ted was lucky that his calls for help were heard
and that there was a creative response that resulted in real
growth for everyone.

*The intensity of the emotional bonding that occurs between
parent and child is a function of what is not happening in the
marriage relationship.* The emptier the marriage, the more the
emotional dance will be between father and daughter or
mother and son or, less frequently, between father and son or
mother and daughter.

A daughter is very often the unconscious surrogate
spouse for her father, reminding him of his wife in her
younger years. Tim and Sheila have been married for 16
years. They have a son and a daughter; the daughter, now 14,
is the older child. The marriage began to go dry in the first
few years of its existence so that when Claire was born, a
strong bonding began to develop between Tim and his
daughter. This is the relationship on which we wish to focus.
By the time she was four years old, Claire had become the
surrogate wife of her father. She pleased him in every way
that she could. She brought him his slippers and the news-
paper when he came home. She sat on his lap. She wanted all
of his attention. She watched his every mood and did
everything she could to make him feel good. The relationship
to the mother turned quite negative, but what mattered was
her Daddy.

All went well until she hit adolescence. She began to have
friends and she began to be away from the house more often.
One evening she stayed out till after her curfew. Both parents
were waiting up but it was Tim who roasted her. He told her
how disgusted he was with her, how she was beginning to act
like a whore. The mother was shocked at the violence of his
reactions and tried her best to stop it, but the other side of the
good father was out and his negative father self was going to
have its say. Claire had not done anything wrong and was

totally shocked by her father's response. She withdrew, as did he, and several months passed in silence between them until the mother finally sought help.

What happened to Tim? He had lived a full and positive bonding with his daughter until this incident occurred. He was father to her good and pleasing daughter and she was mother to his very needy son. Tim's marriage had not worked for many years so there was no way for his vulnerability needs to be met. It had become Claire's job full time. This is an extremely common pattern in parent-child interactions. The bonding remained positive until adolescence when suddenly things changed. Claire began to move out. Without realizing it, Tim's vulnerable child was being left behind. He did not know this, but the negative father was beginning to get stronger and the resentment was beginning to build as he felt more and more deprived. He was feeling more and more betrayed without being able to voice this betrayal in any way. As his negative father enters the scene he begins to withdraw. At first this withdrawal is subtle, but Claire's vulnerable child feels it and she begins to fill the space with more contact with friends who have a new and fresh meaning to her. Thus, the stage is set for the final blowup between them.

When Claire stays out late, Tim's vulnerability is stricken, and since he knows nothing about his inner child, he goes into the rage-filled father as she moves into silent, defiant daughter. There is yet another factor to be considered. Tim has disowned his own sexuality. His relationship to Claire has had a sexual loading without his being aware of it. This is perfectly normal and natural, but many fathers cannot handle sexual feelings in relationship to their daughters. What often happens is that they push off at adolescence and remove themselves from the daughter. They go further into the patriarchy, commonly into a negative, withdrawn, judgmental father, as a way of dealing with their own unconscious sexuality. The sexuality must then be stopped in the daughter. The father, even when there has been a very affectionate relationship, often will begin to withdraw from the daughter, and she will have no idea what has happened, only that something beautiful has been lost.

In Tim's case, he was totally threatened by what he perceived as Claire's burgeoning sexuality, and since his was disowned, this became one of the essential fuels that fed the violence of the bonding pattern. Ultimately, it was the wife who led the family to seek help. It was the marriage that had to be worked with. Thus, the family's bonding patterns pushed them toward growth.

When a Child Is Added to the Family

The addition of a child to an existing family structure is generally, though not always, treated with considerable joy. Unless the child is truly unwanted, or unless there is considerable disturbance in the parents, the new child is a source of pleasure, awe, and attention. At first, this focus of attention is a plus for everyone in the family, except, perhaps, for a sibling who now has to share the attention that was previously directed to it alone. There is often a period after the introduction of a child into the family that resembles the "falling in love" stage of relationship in which everything is wonderful and the parents' inner children feel completely safe. Positive bonding patterns predominate and the discomforts that accompany disowned selves retreat into the background.

At some fairly early stage, however, issues may develop that can lead to negative bonding patterns that, if ignored, can threaten the vitality of the marriage itself. We would like to illustrate how such a pattern might develop.

The early months of a child's life require a fairly intense positive bonding to take place between the mother and child. Without this closeness and intimacy, the child will suffer in a marked way. All later bondings in relationships are parent/child bondings of a similar nature.

It is very important to keep in mind that the inner child is always seeking parents to bond with. This is why vulnerability is so key in triggering the negative bonding patterns. The vulnerable child is always locking into the parent of another person. When that child is threatened in some way, the whole system is threatened and thus the power sides come in to protect the person.

It appears, then, as though later bonding patterns in our lives are meant to serve the same purpose as this initial parent/child bonding, to give the inner child some means of relating to and being protected by the inner parent in another person.

To return to the original mother/child bonding that occurs with the introduction of an infant into a family: the very closeness of this bonding can create problems for many men. Until the baby was born, the woman was far more available to meet the man's own needs. Now she must be shared. Not only that, it is quite likely that she has much less energy available for sharing with the man because the new baby requires a great deal of time and disrupts sleep. Many a woman becomes quite frazzled by the whole experience. Last but certainly not least, the mother's vulnerable child within feels completely safe with the new infant, who adores her unconditionally!

Men also vary a great deal in terms of how they relate to the new child. Some men, an ever-increasing number, throw themselves into the parenting role and participate as enthusiastically as the mother. Many other men, however, simply step back and allow the natural mother/child bonding to take place, they disown their role as parent, and they go about their own business, gradually devoting more and more energy to other parts of their lives such as their work or their favorite leisure activities.

The problem often starts when the man begins to feel deprived. Sometimes he knows that he feels deprived, and other times this happens to him without any kind of awareness at all. Many women in this period of intense bonding with a new baby feel very little sexual desire. For the man, it can be just the opposite. He did not have the baby, nor did he have to go through the birth process. It is also quite possible that he is not getting up at night to feed the baby. In addition to all this, his vulnerability has been touched off by the arrival of a baby who competes with him for attention. He may well want even more sexual contact in order to feel connected to the woman or, perhaps, even to prove his power in the relationship by way of his sexual prowess. Thus, his need system may well be very different from the needs of his wife.

There is another consideration here that often comes into play. The appearance of a first child triggers in most women a powerful energy that has to do with the mothering function. It is a way of being in the world that heretofore was alien to her. Yet, once the child is present, this mothering energy can occupy her totally. There can be a striking change as this mothering function, or self, suddenly overshadows a woman who was previously a fairly carefree spirit or a high-level professional woman. This is a time when a substantial amount of weight may be gained and things feminine may well fly out the window.

How the man relates to all this, whether or not he is aware of his feelings, what he does with them, is going to determine to a considerable extent how the bonding patterns evolve between his wife and himself. Let us look at how some of these patterns might develop.

The New Child

Sharon and Herb have a new child. In the early stages things go well. Both are happy with the child and the new sense of family. Herb initially spends considerable time at home, but soon he has to return to his own work and the family routine begins to develop in a fairly typical way.

Herb, in general, is a very nice guy and tends to be identified with the good father self. Sharon was working before the child came, doing something she did not particularly enjoy, so the child had the secondary benefit of removing her from the workplace. This is one of the harbingers of trouble in a family setting, when the child begins to serve a function that it was not really meant to serve. The new son becomes a kind of escape valve for Sharon, giving her a good excuse for not going to work. These feelings are well beneath the surface for her and for Herb, but they are clearly present.

As time passes, there is a level at which Herb begins to feel betrayed. He has no awareness of this feeling, because it is operating within him well below the surface. The good father in him knows that Sharon needs to be home with the child; this part of him wants this freedom for her.

However, his own inner child does not feel as safe with her as he had before. The needs of this vulnerable child are no longer being met. Sharon has immersed herself in motherhood and Herb feels left out in some way. Herb is a rational man as well as a good father type, and so he ignores these vague feelings and lets things slide.

Herb's vulnerable child also feels betrayed to some extent, because it is obvious that Sharon has no plans to return to work. Now the financial responsibility for the family is entirely on his shoulders. This is okay with the good and responsible father. It is not okay with the vulnerable child, who by now is beginning to feel abandoned in a number of different ways.

Yet another thing is happening that is not feeling too good to Herb. Sharon's sexuality is different. She seemed more sexual before; now she likes to be "snuggled" more. She says that she needs affection, but the sensuality that was present in abundance before is no longer present.

Herb moves ever more deeply into the father role in his behavior toward Sharon, snuggling her as she requests. At a much deeper level, however, a withdrawal begins to take place. Herb is used to dealing with positive feelings and not the negative ones. He has never learned how to react with anger and annoyance, let alone vulnerability. Besides which, his rational self tells him that his feelings are really quite silly. This rational voice makes it even more difficult for Herb to share his feelings and reactions. Over time, this lack of personal reactivity will become increasingly destructive to the relationship.

Why is it that romance can end in relationships where children are present? From our perspective, what happens is that powerful bondings to the children develop and move men and women increasingly into the roles of mother and father. At the same time, many of their other selves become disowned. As responsible mothers and fathers, it becomes more difficult for them to react to one another because they are busier than before. As children get older, the children themselves become an inhibitory influence on spontaneous reactions. More and more energy is spent taking care of the needs of the children, and personal selfishness on the part of the parents becomes more strongly disowned. This is only one scenario, we realize, but it is an amazingly common one.

What unfortunately happens so often in a situation such as the one we have described between Herb and Sharon, is that the stage has been set for the destruction of the marriage, either a literal ending of the marriage or an increasing emotional distancing between the two people. Under the best of circumstances, it can cause a lot of unhappiness. We do not say that this *must* be so, but it certainly happens with great frequency.

In the example above, Herb begins an inner withdrawal. He does not even know that this is happening. He throws himself further into his work; it seems as though his inner pusher is taking over his life in his business. He enjoys his contacts with professional businesswomen very much. Though he is not having any affairs at this point, he looks forward to talking with professional women and being with them. He feels stimulated by their presence.

When he goes home, good father takes over and begins to operate with his son, as well as with Sharon. He enjoys his son, but it is increasingly becoming a matter of form. He watches television more and more, and gradually, over time, a pattern develops in which Sharon goes to bed and he watches television till quite late, always managing a late night meal that becomes a kind of ritual. The gulf between them widens.

What was once a dynamic relationship has become a shell. From the outside it all looks quite normal and Sharon and Herb have an ideal relationship. From the inside, the romance is over. They are "bottled in bondage." They are living a positive bonding pattern in which the good parent of each relates to the obedient child in the other, and all real feeling is disowned.

Fortunately, as we all know, it does not have to go this way. Either Herb or Sharon (or, preferably, both) might bring about a change in the relationship. If Herb became aware of his feelings, he might begin to react. If he was not so afraid of his anger, he might blow up one day and let Sharon know of his dissatisfaction. He might tell Sharon how he feels left out of things, how he misses the intimacy they used to have. After all, children are meant to be children. They are not meant to be the marriage partners of their parents.

In another scenario, Sharon might have lunch with a friend who tells her that she is letting herself go and that she looks terrible. Maybe Sharon has a dream that Herb is making love to another woman, a not uncommon dream in this kind of situation. Maybe she sees Herb fascinated by another woman at a party and she feels jealous. *The identification with bonding patterns makes us forget who we are, if we ever knew who we were in the first place. It is like having amnesia or being asleep. The deeper our sleep, the more shocking is the awakening, which is why so many awakenings take place with one of the partners having a good hot love affair.*

If Sharon and Herb were oriented to personal development and the idea of relationship as teacher, they would have a golden opportunity available to themselves. They are both following family patterns that took root in their own early upbringing. Sharon is re-creating the way in which she was raised by her mother. The children were everything to her mother, just as her child, in a short six months, has become everything to her. Herb's father was ever the nice guy, never angry, never selfish or demanding. It is exactly in this direction that Herb is moving, except that it is not working very well for him. Theirs is a new generation, living in an entirely different world from that of their parents.

Learning from Familial Bonding Patterns

Family bonding patterns can be the instigators of much personal growth and transformation, once we catch hold of them and begin to recognize how they operate within us. We then have the chance to establish new directions in our lives and to create in our personal relationships the kind of love and vitality and romance that we so fervently desire.

It is important to understand that the love that comes from bonding patterns is different than the love that comes from an aware ego that is in touch with the opposing selves. In our relationship to our children, we all walk a difficult line between the blending and fusion that come from the bonding patterns and the separation and clarity that come from awareness and an aware ego. There is no way to eliminate these bonding patterns. They are needed in order to provide the deepest levels of nurturing. They are natural energetic interactions; they are with us forever. We can, however, increasingly separate from them, and with this separation comes a freedom of choice that is otherwise not available. We can learn from each of our relationships. The more clarity that each of us develops in regard to our own bonding patterns, the more consciousness we will bring to our families, friends, and work situations and the less we will be the victims of these patterns.

We have touched on just a few of the types of bonding patterns that occur in families. There are countless variations of family bonding patterns; a comprehensive review of the subject is beyond the scope of this book. However, we have tried to provide enough examples so that readers can be alert to their own family bonding patterns, and can consciously deal with the effects of these patterns as they arise in relationships, within or outside of the family.

Other Bonding Patterns

The awareness that each of us is made up of many different selves is, as we have shown, the key idea in the understanding of bonding patterns. It is only with the separation of the aware ego from the primary selves that one can begin to appreciate the many selves that actually exist within each of us. Only then do we have a chance to examine the multiplicity of selves that are interacting in each of our personal relationships.

We have spoken about the bondings that occur in primary relationships, and we have looked at the evolution of bonding patterns in families. We will now examine bonding patterns in a variety of other relationships.

Therapists and Clients, Teachers and Students

An ever-increasing number of people are showing concern over issues of personal growth. The large number of people who are in some kind of relationship to therapists and teachers brings up a whole new kind of relationship issue and its associated bonding patterns. It is to this issue that we now address ourselves.

The technical name that has long been given to the bonding pattern of client to therapist is the "transference." Historically speaking, transference refers to the projection of unconscious contents from a client to a therapist.

This concept of transference can be extended to include any practitioner of the healing arts. It can be further extended to include the relationship of a client to an attorney or accountant, or to anyone else who offers services as an expert in a particular field. It can be seen in the relationship of an employer and employee. It is in the therapy process, however, that transference has been worked with in a most creative fashion and understood as a necessary part of the treatment process.

Counter-transference refers to the projection of unconscious contents from the therapist onto the client. Generally speaking, any ongoing form of work that is done between a therapist and a client is going to involve the phenomenon of transference and counter-transference, or, as we would call them, characteristic bonding patterns.

In most therapeutic relationships, the bonding pattern that exists is primarily parent/child. If there is no awareness on the part of the therapist, the bonding would be a relatively pure parent/child relationship.

There is no way for the therapist to avoid being identified with the parental self to some degree; no one can be fully aware. However, it is one of the central tasks of therapists and teachers to become aware of where they are identified with these parental selves, or, to put it another way, to become aware of their own counter-transference.

The client enters the therapeutic situation needing help and generally feeling quite vulnerable. The therapist is seen as the one who can bring light and order to a life that is, to some degree, in chaos. The bonding is generally a positive one, and positive attributes are projected onto the therapist.

The projection of unconscious contents is an essential part of personal growth and transformation. Good therapists or teachers recognize the positive nature of this bonding process; at the same time they try to not be identified with the contents being projected onto them. Thus, if the client projects wisdom onto the teacher, the teacher recognizes that the real wisdom lies within the client and that the teacher's job is to help the client gain access to this wisdom.

By accepting the projections as a natural part of the process of personal growth, and by giving the client the necessary tools to understand the different ways of working in, and understanding, transformational work, a natural process ensues in which the client gradually becomes aware of, and embraces, the disowned psychic elements that have been projected out. In this way the projections are gradually withdrawn.

If the therapist or teacher understands bonding patterns, then it is possible to be constantly on the lookout for when one is identified with the parental selves and also when one is feeling vulnerability in relationship to the client.

Once the aware ego of a therapist/teacher separates from the parental side there will be a relationship to vulnerability. This changes the nature of the transaction between the two people. A therapist who is in touch with vulnerability might respond to a client who is leaving therapy by saying: "Oh, I'm sorry! I'm going to miss you" or "I feel bad about that." Being in touch with vulnerability would mean being aware of concerns about money and not acting as though these did not have any real meaning. Being in touch with vulnerability would mean that the therapist would honor the client's personal reactions toward him or her. The clients would not be made to feel that they were being resistant or that their reactions were always a reflection of their own problems.

The denial of vulnerability and neediness on the part of a teacher or therapist, and/or the inability to communicate both of these with awareness automatically means that at some level the therapist/teacher will be playing the game from the power side.

From the client's perspective, the same understanding of bonding patterns is advantageous as well. The client/student generally feels that the teacher/therapist is all-wise and all-knowing. If we can recognize this as a necessary and essential part of the growth process, then we can appreciate the part of ourselves that needs to, and wishes to, surrender to another person because of his or her wisdom and knowledge and personhood in general. The ability to surrender at the proper time, and to remain surrendered as long as is necessary, is a very creative experience for many people in transformational work.

The problem is that not all teachers and therapists know how to handle this kind of surrender. The assumption on the part of the student/client is that the teacher knows all. This, however, is far from the truth. We are all human and we know what we know, and we do not know what we do not know. The unconscious is alive and well within all of us.

This is not a book on professional relationships, nor is it a book on the psychology of the transference. These are highly specialized forms of relationships that happen to be impacting larger and larger numbers of people. We wanted to spend some time discussing the issues surrounding these kinds of bonding patterns, at least to suggest an approach to understanding these relationships that might be useful to the reader. As the last portion of this exploration of bonding patterns, we wish to show you how you can cut to the heart of the bonding patterns in your life by simply looking for the disowned selves that have been activated.

Analyzing the Disowned Selves in Bonding Patterns

As we have shown repeatedly, the disowned self provides the fuel for bonding patterns. *Knowledge of the disowned self systems operating between two people provides the key to understanding the bonding pattern itself.* This represents the translation of some fairly complicated psychological principles into direct, everyday practical applications. Thus, when looking at any bonding pattern between two people, the simplest and most direct entry point into the system is to ask them what disowned selves they carry for one another. The following vignettes illustrate this principle.

We are at a workshop and Al approaches us about his relationship to his son. They have been totally alienated for several years, and it is a very painful situation for him.

Immediately we think in terms of primary selves and disowned selves. What selves are Al and his son each identified with, and what selves do they both disown? Al reports that his son is a very angry young man, verging on the violent. Al, on the other hand, is a very caring, loving, and compassionate man. In fact, he reports, the whole family is more the way Al is. The son is the different one.

How simple is the key to unlocking this painful dilemma! We pointed out to Al how the son lived out Al's disowned self. The son carried all of Al's disowned anger and aggression, everything within him that was "not nice," and lived it out as his primary self. The son was the angry father to Al's child side. Al carried all of the son's loving nature and lived that out as a primary self.

Al could now see a place where he could begin to unravel this heretofore impossibly tangled situation. He needed to become aware that he was identified with his primary selves, his loving and caring nature. Once he can separate from this side, his aware ego can begin to claim that in him which has been rejected: his natural aggression and his "not nice" self. This is work that Al can do on his own or in some kind of therapeutic setting. Our experience has been that when one person in a bonding pattern changes, it often induces in the other person the beginnings of an aware ego. *The understanding of the laws of bonding patterns provides the map. The psychological work, either on one's own or with a therapist, claims the territory.*

Two women at a workshop are friends, and they both report the same story. Their boyfriends smoke dope extensively and do very little else with their lives. Both women have gotten into these kinds of relationships before. Why should this happen repetitively? What is it that makes them, in their terms, co-dependents?

The psychology of selves makes it very clear. Both women are identified with primary selves that have to do with responsibility. It is the responsible mother in them that relates to the men and that is constantly judging these same men. Responsible mothers pull in errant children, and so it is that they are constantly pulling men into their lives who bond with them at the mother/son level. In this way, the women never have the feeling of being taken care of themselves.

The remedy for this repetitive situation is simple. The women must become aware of, and separate from, their responsible mother selves. Then they can begin to claim and care for and honor the parts that have been disowned in them. These would be their own irresponsible selves and their own child sides who need nurturing. Once they begin to care for these selves with an aware ego, it will no longer be necessary to keep pulling them in from the outside.

So often in life we are possessed by things. It may be a person or it may be a material object. A woman passes a Native American shop and in the window is a beautiful squash blossom necklace. She *must* have it, even though she cannot afford it.

Why must she have it? She has entered into a bonding pattern with the necklace. She has become the yearning, victim daughter to the necklace. She has projected her disowned self onto the necklace. It carries magic and spirit for her. It conjures up visions of wisdom and earth energy. She has disowned her own magical spirit, her own inner medicine woman.

We do not judge this phenomenon. We merely comment on it, for it is extremely common. Many things that we purchase are expressions of our disowned selves in addition to being expressions of what we want. When we feel possessed by the object, we may be sure that we are dealing with a disowned self.

A man is possessed by a woman. He is an attorney, a family man, highly rational and highly controlled. What is the woman like? She is, naturally, a pure Aphrodite type. The man gives up family, profession, everything for her, until he has nothing. Then she leaves him.

The more extreme our disowned selves, the more likely we are to be "possessed" by the other person or thing. This man must learn to separate from his proper, conservative self. We do not want him to reject this self, only to separate from it. Then he will have an aware ego that can embrace his own sensual nature, his own playfulness, everything that this "other woman" brought to him. He then will no longer need to be possessed by such a woman on the outside.

Doug has been married for five years. He continues to yearn for Jean, a woman he dated before his marriage. Whenever we see yearning that goes on over time, we suspect that the person is yearning for a disowned self. Doug leads an extremely busy and harassed existence, with no private or quiet time whatsoever. Jean was quiet, introverted, and spiritual. When he left her, he said good-bye to these selves. Thus he continues to live in this painful extroverted, harried state until he is ready to separate from those parts of himself that create this frantic existence. Only then can he embrace his own spiritual, introverted nature. These yearnings can be like a crucifixion, and yet the path out of them is so easily entered upon. We do not say that it is an easy path to follow. We do not minimize the work that has to be done in these situations. Having a map of the territory, however, makes a world of difference to the people involved.

Over and over again we hear people expressing their bonding patterns without having any idea that they are in such a pattern. "I can't stand my brother." "My mother-in-law is really a pill." "I can't stand this or that political figure." "My stepfather is mean, and I hate him." "I hate the Russians." "I hate the Arabs." "I hate the Israelis." "I hate Khomeni, or Reagan, or Bush."

Each of these statements is an expression of one or more disowned selves that throws us into a combination of vulnerability and judgment. If we hate our sister because she is bossy and domineering, and if we don't recognize this as a bonding pattern, we are forever the victim and the persecutor of bossy and domineering women. This goes on forever

until we awaken one day to the reality that all of that
bossiness and dominance is not just out there. It is also a part
of who we are; it is a part of our heritage that has been
disowned. This is a magical moment in the transformational
process, because it is as though we awaken from a deep sleep
and we begin to see each other with eyes that no longer have
blinders on them. We begin to see with the eyes of awareness
rather than the eyes of our primary selves. To live unconsciously in bonding patterns is to live as though asleep.

Strangers on a Train

It can be great fun to see bonding patterns in action when one
is not the least bit involved. In the spring of 1987, we taught
for two months in Australia. During this time we took the
Indian Pacific train ride across Australia from Melbourne to
Perth.

We had the same dinner companions assigned to our
table for the two days we spent on the train. One was an older
woman, a native of Bali, who been living in Australia for a
number of years. She was a very imposing woman, both
physically and psychologically, and she was the obvious
matriarch of her family. On the train she had met her
travelling companion, a shy, introverted Japanese woman
who was travelling in Australia for her two-month yearly
holiday.

The two women were perfect disowned selves of each
other, and they lived out a marvelous bonding pattern in
which the older woman was clearly the power mother to the
younger one's dutiful daughter. The Balinese woman was
identified with power and disowned her diffidence; the
Japanese woman identified with her diffidence and disowned
her power.

During lunch one day, we had finished our meal and the
waiter came to our table asking whether we wanted dessert.
He asked us first, and, after we had responded, he then asked
the younger Japanese woman if she wanted dessert. She

spoke English relatively well, clearly had done a considerable amount of travelling alone, and obviously knew how to take care of herself. Immediately, however, the older woman said to the waiter: "No, she doesn't want dessert—but I'll have some." It happened so quickly and so automatically that it was literally as though she were possessed, as though some alien entity had spoken through her and taken over the situation. With considerable embarrassment and uncomfortable laughter, the younger woman said that she *did* want dessert. At this point the older woman said: "Oh, I'm sorry."

Though we did not know the details of her life, it was clear that our older woman was very much an "in charge" lady. She had immediately found her natural travelling companion, someone with whom she could bond comfortably and enter into her natural style of relationship. These bonding patterns are like putting on an old shoe that fits and that we are used to wearing all the time. The disowned selves set up an energetic vacuum that pulls in their particular energy. The patterns pull upon us like the force of gravity, and developing an aware ego that can separate us from them is really going against gravity. Most of the time it takes real work to unbond. It seldom happens naturally.

The Attorney and the Judge

Margaret is a judge in a large eastern city. One day there appears in her courtroom a woman attorney who has established a reputation amongst the judges of the court system. This attorney is able to drive judges crazy by behaving like an aggressive, rebellious daughter. She never does anything serious enough to warrant her eviction from the courtroom, but she skirts the edge with skill and efficiency.

From our perspective, she creates a perfect bonding pattern. She identifies with her rebellious daughter self who dances with the stern and patriarchal father or mother of the judge who happens to be sitting on the bench on any particular day. Everyone dreads having her come into the courtroom, except her own clients; since she wins most of her cases, they are very happy with her. She fully disowns her "establishment" self.

In Margaret's courtroom, the same pattern emerges. Margaret is thrown into her critical and judgmental mother and she feels quite trapped by the situation. The lawyer wears sexually provocative clothing and behaves in every respect like the provocative and rebellious daughter that she is. Margaret finds herself forcefully defending the rules and the expectations of the "establishment."

However, Margaret knows something about bonding patterns. She knows that she is hooked in some way and she seeks help to find out what is happening. During the first session, the therapist facilitates the part of her that is the rebellious daughter.

It is only by watching or experiencing this kind of work that one can have any real appreciation of how real and autonomous these different selves can be. They are not just "parts." They behave and act like real, live people, and one can observe total changes in the physical appearance of the person who is being facilitated.

Margaret had a powerful "rebellious daughter" in her that had been very much disowned. This self had a lot to say about the judges and how she felt about the fact that Margaret was a judge. This self was very sensual and manipulative and was dying to come out in Margaret's life.

It took only a few minutes for Margaret to understand the process that was occurring between herself and the attorney. Since Margaret had disowned her "rebellious daughter," life had of course brought it to her. Life always brings us our disowned selves, over and over and over again, until we recognize the outer people who carry these selves as teachers for us. Margaret knew that she had something to learn from this attorney, despite the harsh and negative feelings that she had toward her. By becoming aware of and embracing this self, the fuel for the bonding was no longer present. Margaret's "rebellious daughter" no longer needed to be projected.

The following week in the courtroom was an amazing experience for Margaret. When the attorney came in, Margaret had no particular reactions to her. She was no longer bothered by the provocative behavior in the least. The attorney had no one to play off against. She was totally identified with her rebellious daughter, and when the judge was no longer in critical parent, the attorney lost her power. From a very aggressive and successful attorney, she started to fumble and become quite ineffectual. Over the next few days her performance in the courtroom deteriorated markedly.

When one person in a bonding pattern is able to withdraw from the dance floor of bonding, there is going to be a major shift on the other side. If no consciousness had emerged out of this experience for the attorney, then no doubt she would have found some other arena in which to play out her rebellious daughter self. She does have an opportunity, however, that she otherwise would not have had. Margaret's shift gives her a chance to discover something about herself. Whether someone can take advantage of such an opportunity depends on whether or not there is some kind of opening in the person to personal growth and development.

One sees frequently a situation in which a spouse leaves a marriage and ends up in another marriage, and possibly many more, living out the same bonding patterns that had been lived out in the first marriage. He (or she) keeps wondering what is wrong with women (or with men), rather than finding out what is disowned that is bringing in the same kind of relationship over and over again.

The Issue of Betrayal

How often we have seen marriages of fifteen to twenty years that are suddenly broken by an affair on the part of the husband or wife. The other feels totally betrayed, but the soil of that betrayal was the fifteen years of living out the good and responsible parents and children to each other without any realistic kind of communication process. The implicit promise in the positive bonding interaction is that the good parents and good children will always be there for one another.

In these cases there is no way of knowing what was really going on between the couple. Good mothers and fathers do not admit to the possibility of discomfort, do not share negativity, and keep a wide variety of other, less acceptable, selves shut up securely in the attic. They do not even know about these selves because they have been disowned. When these selves break out, the bonding pattern dissolves and the relationship is in for a big change.

When one is in this kind of bonding, whether it be with a spouse, a family member, or a friend, there is often an intense feeling of loyalty. Sometimes, however, there is the opposite feeling of wanting to hurt and betray the other person.

Rhonda wants to get a job. Her husband tells her it isn't necessary because they have more than enough money and they would have to pay more taxes than her job was worth. Later she wants to take a class at a university at night. He tells her he is worried about her at night. It seems too dangerous. Rhonda disowns her own power and her ability to think. Again the dutiful daughter wins out as she gives in to his logic and rational mind. Six months later he leaves her for another woman, and she discovers that he has been having an ongoing relationship with her for almost three years. She naturally feels totally betrayed and is ready to kill.

Aware egos do not experience betrayal. It is the innocence of the good mother-father and the good and obedient son-daughter and the implicit promises they make that leads to the experience of betrayal. Thus, even Rhonda's betrayal becomes the vehicle for growth as her bonding patterns are cut by her husband's abandonment.

A Final Look at Bonding

We are well aware of the fact that we are greatly simplifying complex life situations. Our aim in this, however, is to give a picture of universal and natural bonding patterns and how they influence our lives. Our hope is that you will recognize yourselves and other people in these examples, and that out of this awareness a different kind of process can emerge.

We have tried in these two chapters to give you an overview of the bonding process as it is found in many different life situations. These bondings are constantly present, and the more you become aware of them, the more of them you will discover. *Keep in mind the basic idea that these bonding patterns are a normal and natural phenomena. Occurring without awareness, they give rise to fixed patterns of thought, feeling, and behavior in our relationships. Once we have awareness, then a magic door opens to us and we have the opportunity to step through it and to explore an amazing array of patterns that are operating within us in our relationships.* We hope these chapters have helped to create a focus with which you will be able to identify and examine some of the patterns of your own lives.

PART III

Living in
Relationship

6

Attractions and Affairs

There is a most memorable interchange in the Kazantzakis novel, *Zorba the Greek*. Zorba is talking to the narrator of the book, a rational writer who is fearful about getting into a relationship with the deliciously attractive village widow. He says: "You don't want any trouble! And pray, what do you want, then? Life is trouble, death, no."

This pretty much sums up the question of attractions and affairs in primary relationship. If we are alive, we are going to be attracted to people on many different levels. We may be drawn physically, emotionally, psychologically, spiritually, or any combination of the above. How we handle these attractions is one of the most complex issues of primary relationship. So, we are bound to agree with Zorba. Life is trouble; death is not. You will see, however, how a knowledge of the selves and of bonding patterns can help you to navigate in these particularly difficult waters and how these, too, can help you to use your relationships as teachers.

To begin with, our different selves feel very differently from one another when it comes to our attractions and affairs. Our sexual and lustful selves are generally not at all

161

monogamous; they are frequently attracted to other partners, and they generally want to be sexually involved. Our
free spirit, in a similar fashion, wants to do whatever it wants
to do whenever it wants to do it. It does not like to feel
imprisoned by the boundaries of relationship. Our selfish
side wants to do what gives it pleasure. Our rational and
"New Age" sides may feel that jealousy is inappropriate, that
personal freedom is everything, and for this reason anything
that anyone does is just fine. For these selves, life should be
excitingly spontaneous, free of constraints, and unconcerned
with consequences.

On the other hand, our inner conservative wants us to
have nothing to do with affairs and, depending on our
background, might even be judgmental if there is any hint of
attractions. The responsible parts of ourselves will generally
reject any kind of feeling or behavior that would even suggest
that we might not be behaving responsibly in our primary
relationship. The good father and good mother also would
have a difficult time with outside involvements. We might
also have a strong ethical side that rejects affairs, and possibly
even a strong control side that refuses to allow any kind of
attraction to be experienced.

We have only just begun to see how complicated this can
become. In a wonderful Catch-22 fashion, our inner critic
may criticize us because we are having affairs or even feeling
attractions. It might, however, also criticize us because we
are not feeling attractions or because we do not have the
courage to have affairs. We can even be drawn into affairs
without feeling particularly attracted. Our pleaser can involve us in an affair for no other reason than the fact that he or
she could not say no because this might mean hurting the
other person. The son or daughter side of us might get
involved to have someone take care of us, and the power side
might get involved largely to dominate someone else. Along
with all of these is the driving power of our sexuality,
amplified and supported by many of these different selves.

On yet another level, we might find ourselves drawn to

someone who touches a very deep soul space in us or brings forth intense feelings of love that we have never experienced before. Our inner child may feel sparked by someone outside of our primary relationship. Our magical child may be cued off by someone with a rich imagination and an intuitive nature. Our playful child might be met by someone who is capable of bringing out this part of ourselves.

Many of our selves, then, may be powerfully attracted to the idea of an affair. However, one of the most powerful selves that needs to be considered in the whole issue of attractions and affairs is the vulnerable child, and he or she has a whole different kind of experience of this matter.

A fine kettle of fish! How are any of us even to begin to deal with these intricacies of the human psyche? Where can we possibly turn to try to sort out these complex conflicts and begin to make decisions that truly represent who we are, rather than decisions that represent the automatic and unconscious responses of the primary selves who are currently running the show? The more aware we are of these different selves, the more direct experience we have of them, the more real choice we have about what we do in life. It is not up to us to tell you how to live your life and what is the right or wrong way to behave. What we can say is that the more awareness and experience you have of who you are, the better off you will be in making these decisions, and the more you will be in control of your life and your environment. Let us begin our examination of attractions and affairs from the standpoint of the vulnerable child. We have chosen to start with the child because of its very important place in relationship in general and primary relationship in particular.

The Vulnerable Child in Relationship

The vulnerable child, as we have said before, is one of the most essential ingredients in a truly complete relationship, for the child is the basis of our deepest intimacy. There may be many wonderful points of contact between two people. The couple may be able to function beautifully together physically, emotionally, and professionally, but, without the child, something indefinable is missing, and there is always a yearning for something more. It is this yearning that signals the absence of the vulnerable child.

The vulnerable child, from our perspective, is the gateway to the soul. If one's child is not available, soul contact is very difficult with another human being.

There are many times in any relationship when the vulnerable child withdraws. This is natural in the ebb and flow of life. When bonding patterns develop, as shown in previous chapters, the child usually runs for cover, and there is a feeling of emptiness and loss. The reconnection to our vulnerable child and its reappearance in the relationship is always a time for rejoicing.

However, it is a most unusual vulnerable child who can tolerate the pain of a partner who has other relationships. The inner child is extremely sensitive. Although we may not know that our partner is having an affair, our vulnerable child senses it at some level and automatically begins a process of withdrawal from the partner. It is this astounding sensitivity that the child brings to the relationship, and it is the same sensitivity that causes it to withdraw. Our rational mind may explain our fears or doubts away, but it cannot convince the child.

It follows that if we want a truly deep commitment and if we want the child to remain a part of our relationship, we will have to find some way to assure its safety. Whether or not this can be done in a non-monogamous relationship is the real question. Our experience so far is that the vulnerable child cannot handle the reality of the other person having other partners, particularly when those relationships become sexual. At this point, the child withdraws at some level.

We must remember that the child is unimpressed with

theories. It wants to be loved and it wants to feel safe. From its point of view, we can have any kind of non-monogamous relationship we wish. It, however, will not participate.

Once the child disappears, there are a variety of ways in which we can make things all right. We can shift over to the sexual track and decide that two can play this game; in this way we open ourselves to different sexual experiences. We can identify with our rational mind and develop a philosophy and rationale as to why monogamy destroys relationships and prevents growth. Whatever subpersonalities we shift into, the child will be gone.

Staying with the child means staying with one's pain. This is the hardest thing in the world to do. But staying with the pain might truly make things right again by keeping the vulnerable child in the relationship and allowing the relationship to continue its teaching. This does not mean, however, that we become victims, suffering mightily at our betrayal by our partner. It simply means that we stay with the process and see where it will lead us.

Everyone Has Attractions

Attractions are a natural part of our everyday existence. What we do with them and how we handle them is the real issue.

Of course, as we have described briefly in the last section, there are other parts of us that feel quite different from our vulnerable child. Our sexual selves, which might include (amongst others) Aphrodite, the satyr, the playboy, and the open marriage or free love advocate, all yearn for multiple partners. These selves are extremely important and carry with them much energy and a high intensity of feeling. Their attractions do not lessen just because we wish, from an aware ego, to engage in an intense, consciousness-enhancing relationship that includes the vulnerable child. Needless to say, this poses quite a problem. Talk about embracing the opposites!

None of us can deny these selves to save our relationships. This would just put us back in the position of disowning some parts in favor of others. And it does not necessarily
work. The fact that we would rather not acknowledge a self
does not in any way make it disappear. If we feel very strong
and deep attractions for other people and try to stuff them
down into the unconscious, these feelings simply go underground and begin to operate in the dark. When these feelings
operate in the dark we do not see or know what is going on.
But our partners and our friends usually do. We may not
notice the way we stared or blushed or stopped talking when
someone attractive came by, but those others with us are
very likely to see. Most definitely, the vulnerable child of our
partner knows, and knows immediately.

These attractions can range from a mild interest and
delight to an intense fascination. They may happen all the
time or just occasionally. When attractions are extremely
intense and become a preoccupation, it is usually a sign that
something serious is missing in the relationship or that
something important is not being talked about. The following is a classic example of a strong attraction signalling that
something is missing from a relationship.

After many years of marriage, Joan became less thoughtful of Peter and stopped planning exciting things for them to
do together. Their children were teenagers and they oc-
cupied her completely. At this time, Peter was facing the
added financial pressures of college tuition and emotional
pressures at work. It seemed as though his life had no fun in it
anymore. He found himself intensely attracted to a young
woman at work. She was bright, happy and extroverted, and
she always seemed to be having a good time. He thought
about her constantly and wished that he had the courage to
have an affair with her.

Something is missing in Peter's marriage, and he is
drawn to it when he sees it elsewhere. Somewhere along the
way he has lost his natural connection to his own playfulness.
He has become identified with being responsible and seri-

ous. Before he met Joan, he had no connection with his own playfulness and fun-loving side. Joan brought this out in him. He needed her to bring this out in him, because he had never fully embraced it as a part of himself.

Now, his playful child, who had been cared for by Joan, is no longer considered important and feels abandoned. Joan's attention has switched to the couple's children; she has fun with them and with her girlfriends. He misses this element of lightness in his own life, and he is naturally drawn to this energy elsewhere. His attraction to the young woman in his office is intense. He spends much time daydreaming about her and wondering what life would be like with her instead of with Joan.

Most of us are used to thinking about attractions on the basis of our physical feelings, and these can certainly become very powerful in these situations. However, the fascination and power of this attraction is at least in part a function of the fact that the young woman is an expression of a disowned self in him with which he desperately wants to connect.

Attractions that are based on disowned selves can become extremely powerful. These kinds of attractions can become obsessions that will not release us despite all of our attempts to extricate ourselves. They can often monopolize our energies, inexorably drawing us out of our current relationship. They can draw us into behavior that is very destructive or non-productive, or they can open us up to a very new and creative kind of relationship. Let us look at a few examples of this kind of disowning and see how the relationships might be impacted.

Laura had lived out her Aphrodite, her sexual self, during her adolescence. She was sexually active, and she loved to take drugs, dance, and stay out all night. However, the disapproval that this elicited from her classmates was distressing to her basically sensitive nature. After graduation, she left town, another self in her took over, and she disowned the Aphrodite self that had been such a major part of her life.

Laura, or more accurately the proper woman in Laura, married a quiet, sensible man who was completely out of touch with his own sexuality. They lived a life devoid of the excitement of her past. She was able to maintain this lifestyle for a number of years until she met Ned, her tennis teacher.

Ned was the disowned self that she had left behind. He romanced all the ladies, drank, took drugs, and generally acted the tempter. Laura found herself hopelessly attracted to Ned. She began an affair with him even though this put her marriage and her hard-won social status at risk. She found herself taking drugs again, and she found herself sneaking money away from the household accounts to give to Ned. Although she kept trying to break the relationship and to "reform" herself for a second time, the pull to this disowned self was irresistible.

When we look at marriage relationships in general, we often discover that it was a particular self in a person who got married. Sometimes the man or woman is aware of what is being sacrificed or disowned. At other times there is no awareness on any level, and the disowning is complete. *The more extreme the disowning process, the more extreme is the attraction likely to be to someone who carries the disowned energy.* These kinds of attractions happen as a way of forcing us to meet, and eventually embrace, our disowned selves.

Let us contrast this particular attraction and affair with the attraction that Henry feels. Henry is a strongly sexual man who is in touch with this sexuality. He is like many men: he loves women. He notices attractive women wherever he is, and he feels a thrill and a desire to have sexual relations with them. This attraction is non-specific but strong.

From time to time Henry experiences discomfort with these sexual feelings because he knows that his wife feels very vulnerable with them, but he knows that if he tries to deny them, all the sexuality disappears from his life. Henry walks the line between honoring his attractions and acting upon them. Because he does this, they do not gain power in his life. His sexual self is a part of his life and a part of his relationship to his wife. Unlike Laura's, it is not disowned.

Henry relates to his wife from an aware ego, honoring his sexuality but protecting their relationship and staying related to the needs of her vulnerable child (and his, too). He enjoys the feeling of being attracted and does not feel compelled to hide it, but, at this point in his life, his choice is to remain monogamous.

Attractions Are a Part of the Process

Attractions perform a number of important functions in most of our lives. First of all, they bring great vitality with them. If we never experience sexual attractions, it is quite likely that we have disowned an important self and have thereby cut off a major source of psychic energy.

Secondly, they break bondings, and they break them with a vengeance! There are few things that catch the attention of a partner with the intensity and immediacy of a good solid attraction to someone else. Thirdly, they alert us to what is missing within ourselves or within the relationship.

It is extremely important, therefore, to make our attractions a part of the process of relationship. This does not mean that we must compulsively comment every time we notice somebody attractive. It is unlikely that a continuous commentary of this type is coming from an aware ego; it is more likely to be a power play from a controlling mother or controlling father. Sharing attractions from an aware ego almost always involves some hesitation and discomfort. When we love someone, we usually wish to spare this person pain, and we always risk hurting the other when we talk of our attractions to someone else. In addition, most of us have a guilty child within who fears that somehow when we hurt our partner with this revelation of our perfidy, we will be punished in return. Last, but definitely not least, our vulnerable child fears abandonment every time that we are brave enough to discuss our attractions with our partner.

However, attractions do play an important part in the process and sharing them does help to move things along, although sometimes the movement can be fairly uncomfortable. For instance, attractions break bondings. When a couple is cozily bonded, this bonding will usually be unconscious; they will not be aware of the fact that they are bonded. If one or the other (or both, for that matter) start to experience attractions outside the relationship, this is the relationship's way, if you will, of signalling that something is off in the way they are connecting to each other.

If they are in a solid bonding pattern, they will try to ignore the attractions and work things out on their own. These attractions then tend to become stronger and more numerous. Perhaps something will happen to break open the bonding pattern but, if nothing else works, talking about the attractions forces the issue. When we talk about our attractions, we automatically move out of good parent or pleasing child and must look to the totality of our selves and the complexity of the relationship. We are no longer playing it safe and exposing only our more reassuring selves to one another. In this way, we begin to become aware of and separate from the bonding pattern with which we have been identified.

The alternative to sharing our feelings and fantasies is to begin to lead a secret life. What happens here is that we live with a partner, but more and more time is spent living inside our own head. Our secret fantasy life can easily become more interesting and intense than the actual relationship in which we are involved. This can even develop to a point where our partner is tolerated sexually by virtue of the fact that the fantasy partner or partners are substituted for our real partner during sexual relations.

This secret life is a very natural phenomenon that develops in primary relationships. As it grows, we generally feel guilty about it and so we have an even stronger motivation to keep it private. It is obvious that at some point, the real relationship is going to suffer and eventually a serious deterioration in the quality of relationship will take place. Intimacy in relationship cannot live forever alongside an ever-growing secret life that is directed toward other men and women.

On the other side we have relationships in which a decision is made by the couple to live out their sexuality freely, so long as there is some measure of discretion involved. Sometimes there is the added proviso that the partners not become seriously involved with another person, and that if this happens they will tell each other. We are very pragmatic about relationship. Our feeling is that what works, works. There are many people living in such open relationships who are very pleased about the way they work. Many of these relationships also come to an end. Interestingly enough, we have not met very many people who have made the choice for an open relationship in a second marriage.

The main issue in these kinds of open relationships is the status of the vulnerable child. We have spoken of this before. Many of our different selves absolutely love the idea of an open relationship. The vulnerable child does not feel this way at all and, generally speaking, will gradually remove him- or herself from the partner. This has an interesting effect, because as the child is removed, some deeply satisfying energetic exchange between ourselves and our partners disappears. This is a physical as well as a psychological fact and, as this energetic exchange disappears, we are more and more starved for outside relationships that might bring it to us.

Sometimes the awareness that one's partner is attracted elsewhere can act as a powerful motivation for growth. Most of us can use this motivation to look at aspects of ourselves that we would prefer to ignore, those selves that we find truly objectionable. We can even use it to help us take the next step in our own evolution of consciousness quickly, lest we end up taking it alone. This may not be the world's most noble motivation, but it certainly works!

Cindy and Clyde are girlfriend and boyfriend. Cindy is a gifted academic student and, as we might we expect, Clyde is much more into pleasure and non-academic pursuits. He is helping to make a film and has to spend some time away from her. Cindy is very jealous and is convinced he will have an affair with one of the actresses. There is no real evidence that this is going to happen, but we may safely assume that he felt strong attractions toward some of these actresses. So long as Cindy identifies with her academic self and disowns her own actress self (that in her which is concerned with beauty, makeup, clothing, appearance), she will always be strongly jealous of Clyde and will literally drive him to the actress type. If Cindy can become aware of the actress as a disowned part of herself, her jealousy of Clyde will change and he will feel less attracted to the actresses in his life. From his side, if he were able to admit more openly that he was attracted to one or more of these actresses, the issue would be much more natural and neutralized between them. By not admitting his own feelings, Cindy is forced to carry them for the two of them.

Talking about attractions helps us to clarify aspects of the relationship that are not working well. If Peter were to talk to his wife about his attraction to the young woman in his office, they would most probably go on to discuss her bonding to their children and his responsible father bonding to his family. He could then tell her of his unhappiness at being neglected and his irritation at being taken for granted. His wife might let him know that she, too, had been feeling left out, that she felt he was preoccupied with their finances and was always working, and that she was upset because they never took time for themselves, time to have fun as they had in the past. Entire areas that they had politely covered over would come to the surface for examination and, ultimately, some form of resolution. Such discussions are painful, but avoiding them gradually erodes the relationship.

So often in relationship, couples refuse to fight and show anger or upset because the children are around. If we wait till the children are not around to have our fights and display our anger, we can wait for decades before we ever get things off our chest. Strong bonding patterns invariably have strong anger underneath. We are not suggesting that the expression of anger should become a way of life in a home. We are simply saying that anger is natural and that it needs to come out when it needs to come out.

It is important to realize, too, that as the love energy disappears from the primary relationship, it can lock onto one or more of the children, and when this happens, they begin to develop an importance that does not properly belong to them. So often in family dynamics, as we have seen, one or more of the children develops a sense of self-importance that is extreme and unnatural. One of the reasons this happens is that the son or daughter becomes a surrogate wife or husband for one of the parents. This can be an excellent motivation for parents to develop a more effective primary relationship or perhaps, if this is impossible, to separate from one another.

It is always frightening to the vulnerable child when we open up new areas for exploration, talk about some part of the relationship that is not working well, or discuss an issue without knowing where the talk will lead. The child is usually uncomfortable to hear about our partner's realities, whatever these might be. But this is what keeps relationships alive and what brings about new growth.

As we have said, attractions tend to bring up our disowned selves. In the example of Laura, the disowned self was a frightening one. She felt unable to deal with her Aphrodite sexuality in any way other than disowning it. Her inability to talk of her attraction kept her from bringing her disowned sexuality into the marriage and locked her into acting upon it in a long-term and generally uncomfortable affair. If she had been using her marriage relationship as a teacher rather than as a safe refuge from the perils of her sexuality, she might have shared her attraction to Ned with her husband. Together, they might have traced it back to her disowned sexuality and, together, they might have worked out a way to bring this into the marriage. The apparently fatal attraction might have led to a growth spurt and an enriching of the marital relationship.

There is always a risk and there is always fear when we are brought face to face with a disowned self. There is, indeed, the possibility that Laura's husband would have been threatened by her sexuality and would not have tolerated it. This would have left Laura with the option of disowning her sexuality anew or deciding that she did not wish to live her life without it and, therefore, ending her marriage. It would force a decision from an aware ego.

It requires a good deal of courage for most of us to own up to our attractions, to explore them, and to dig down into their roots. The end of the process is not predictable, which is why, when we are in a bonding pattern and fully committed to holding on to the relationship at all costs, we do not like to enter into these threatening discussions.

There is always the possibility that we will discover that our differences are irreconcilable, and that the relationship must end. But it would be an honest ending that involved two aware egos, and we would each have learned something new. We would have continued our own growth process. Each of these explorations into consciousness brings its own reward by furthering our individual evolutionary process.

The Role of Affairs in Relationship

Affairs, aside from the pure physical and emotional pleasure that they bring, serve a wide variety of functions for people. They also affect the primary relationship in many different ways. There are times when an affair will end a relationship. One's vulnerable child rarely forgives and never forgets. Once that child's trust has been violated, it is rather difficult to reinstate the level of trust and the intensity of relationship that had preceded the affair. However much we try to convince or cajole, the child will not be brought back into the relationship in the same way once it has been betrayed. It will remain wary for quite some time.

There are, of course, exceptions to this as we shall see.

These exceptions are generally found in people who have developed a deeper understanding of themselves and their partners and who can begin to really nurture their own inner children in a new and very special way.

If a couple is in a classically bonded relationship, an affair may help to balance the energies and maintain the status quo, or it may help to break the bonding pattern. In the first case, the affair protects the bonding. Take, for example, Dan, who lives his life at home in the responsible father bonded to the needy child in his wife and in his children. Dan is always providing nurture, help, guidance, and money, but his needy child receives no care.

In order to balance this, Dan becomes involved with a woman who wants nothing more than to take care of him and make him happy. He carries on a lifelong relationship with this woman. This affair, then, allows Dan to remain in his bonded marriage as the responsible father while his needy child receives his nurturing and emotional support elsewhere.

Dan might receive the same nourishment from his office administrator or nurse or secretary. Not all such affairs are overtly sexual; some are energetic bonding patterns that can be very much like marriages. Unless the other partner is quite sensitive to the meaning of such relationships, no fuss is made unless or until the affair becomes a sexual one. Our needy children must be cared for, and we will find some way for this to happen, whether we do this consciously or unconsciously.

Affairs can also act in such a way as to break bondings. Let us take John as an example. He is exactly the same type of responsible father as Dan. His affair takes another course. He becomes involved with a very sensual, free woman who awakens in him his own disowned sexuality. The integration (or taking back) of this sexuality changes him and breaks the dominance of the responsible father who has always ruled his life. This, in turn, begins to break the bonding with his wife. He returns home and makes new demands upon the marital relationship. Since he would no longer be identified with the responsible father, he finally tells his wife that he is dissatisfied with their sex life, that he wants her to take more responsibility for decisions in the family, and that he wants her to get a job and help out with the financial burden. He has also learned about feelings and about his own vulnerability in the freer atmosphere of the affair. Knowing this enables him to talk with his wife differently and be sensitive to her feelings in a way that had been impossible from his position as the responsible father. This, in turn, allows new selves to emerge in his wife who, up until now, has been kept in a dependent daughter position.

In this example, the affair would have broken a bonding pattern, released much new energy, and resulted in a totally changed marital relationship. It would have precipitated a period of growth rather than preserved the status quo.

Sometimes an affair can move us along in our evolution of consciousness when our marriage has come to some sort of roadblock. Jack, for instance, is another responsible father type. His life consists of taking care of wife, children, office help, dogs, and whatever else is within his orbit. He is highly principled and strongly monogamous in his philosophy of marriage.

At a party, Jack meets Gwen and gets pulled into an affair over which he seems to have very little control. She is a very sensual woman, different from anyone he has ever known. On a night that he has been with her he dreams that all the displaced persons and minority groups of Central Europe are returning home from their dispersion around the world.

It is clear from this dream that Jack's involvement with Gwen has touched him deeply and is having a strongly healing effect on him. The minorities and displaced persons are the parts of himself that have had n , home, and this relationship is helping them to find their rightful place in his psyche. Jack's involvement with Gwen stayed an involvement. He ultimately remained in the marriage, though it was a very different marriage than it had been before. The drive toward consciousness is an intense one, and if a particular relationship does not support that drive, it is natural for another relationship to come along that does support this drive toward a greater awareness.

There is usually an intense pull to have an affair when something within wishes us to break form and move ahead. As we have seen, there is an intelligence inside of us that pushes us forward on a path of ever-increasing awareness. This is a natural evolutionary process that demands movement.

On the other hand, there is also a natural process that works against this evolutionary process, one that aims to protect the status quo at any cost. An affair can serve either purpose. It can help us to maintain the status quo and shore up a relationship that does not support us in our entirety but is one that, nevertheless, we do not wish to lose. Or, an affair can be the catalyst that introduces new selves, releases new energies, and either changes or ends our current relationship, thereby leading us into a new phase of our evolution of consciousness.

Margie and Mac had been married for many years. They had married at a time when women were expected to give up their own lives and become mothers and wives. They loved each other dearly, but once Margie gave up her schooling and her plans for a professional life, they slipped into a strong father/daughter bonding, with Mac as the competent good father and decision-maker and Margie living out the role of the helpless daughter.

Margie, an intelligent and perceptive woman, could not keep her power and competence disowned forever, and she began an affair that lasted for some time. In this relationship she was the guiding force and her lover relied greatly upon her intelligence and her understanding of human relationships. Sensing that there was a good deal more to the affair than met the eye, Margie entered therapy. After some time she reclaimed her own power in her relationship with Mac, and the bonding pattern that had been entered into so long ago was broken.

Mac gave many indications that he did not want to be told

of the affair, and Margie obliged. Realizing that his vulnerable child could not tolerate hearing about it, she never did tell him directly about her affair. At some level she was most assuredly protecting herself too.

The marriage, however, had become a marriage again. As the disowned selves were integrated, the father/daughter bonding was no longer the predominant mode of relating and there was a return of the love that they had originally felt earlier in their relationship. As Margie said when the bonding had broken, "I had forgotten how much I loved him!"

How do we reconnect in a relationship after one partner has had an affair and the other has found out about it? As we have said, there are ways in which to resume a truly intimate relationship, complete with vulnerable children, even after there has been a betrayal of trust and the vulnerable child has been hurt.

Bill and Edna's relationship was committed to growth from the beginning, and the sharing of their psychological processes was important to both of them. They needed to tell each other about all their important relationships. For a period of time it was necessary for them to live in different cities, but their connection remained deep and they were in constant contact with one another.

One day Edna sensed that something was very wrong, and she telephoned Bill to ask whether anything had happened. He had actually become intensely involved with another woman, but he was ashamed to tell Edna, so he denied everything and suggested that she might be projecting her own feelings upon him. He was reacting to Edna from a combination of guilt and judgment. She, in turn, was alternately feeling abandoned and expressing judgment, a not uncommon pattern. The bonding was complete, and they were both miserable.

When Bill finally realized what was going on, he spoke to Edna about what had happened. He spoke with awareness rather than from his guilty son (which only would have made matters worse). They looked together into what had happened and realized that they had been in a mother/son bonding for some time, and that the affair had broken the bonding. As a result of their serious commitment to a conscious relationship, and after a lot of personal work, they were able to resume their relationship at an even greater depth. They recognized that their initial mother/son bonding had precipitated the affair and that the affair had broken the bonding. They both now had an appreciation of the sensitivity of their vulnerable children and were aware of just how much these children knew. The relationship had taught each of them much more about themselves.

These last examples have shown how an affair can precipitate a new awareness or even lead one to a new level of consciousness in a current relationship. However, there are many times when the growth process is aborted by an affair, when the pain of the vulnerable child is too great and the child withdraws forever from that particular relationship that, like Humpty Dumpty, can never be fixed. We have seen quite a bit of this, particularly in the years of experimentation with open marriages. For many people, there was an initial excitement about the idea of an open marriage, but when they actually opened their own marriages, something about it often did not work. It seemed as though the vulnerable child could not understand the principle of an open marriage, and it withdrew from the relationship altogether. A fair percentage of these marriages ended in divorce.

If the vulnerable child refuses to return to a relationship, and if the incident is used as a teaching, then the partners can face the fact that the particular relationship is over and they are free to continue on the relational path with someone else. They are in a position to begin a more conscious relationship with the next person, based upon their previous learning.

Unfortunately, however, the protector/controller sometimes steps in after a relationship is terminated in this way and withdraws the child (and them) into a safe and protected space, thereby ending the process and keeping them safely removed from relationship forever.

As for the attractions themselves, it is clear that they are a natural part of our lives whether we are in or out of a primary relationship, so we may as well accept them. This will probably deprive our critics of a particularly rewarding area of criticism, one that they have counted upon since puberty and one that enables them to make us guilty children quite easily. But we need not fear; our critics are extremely resourceful and will certainly find some other focus for their efforts.

When attractions are long-term and intense, as we have described earlier in this chapter, we may well find ourselves leading a secret life in our heads, a secret life of fantasy. When this goes on for too long, the relationship must suffer because we become increasingly withdrawn from our partners. It is a highly paradoxical situation. The more attached we are to our partners, the deeper the bonding in the relationship, the harder it is to share these kinds of feelings and fantasies. Yet, the act of sharing them is one of the key ways in which we can separate from these patterns. As we have said, we are all sensual and sexual human beings and these kinds of feelings will simply not remain confined to the bedrooms of our primary relationships. They are with us for life and must accompany us wherever we go, no matter how much discomfort this may cause us, and no matter how deep our love and commitment may be to our primary partners.

Now that we have studied bonding patterns, how they interfere with intimacy in relationship, and how we can learn from them, let us turn our attention to some of the ways in which we can enhance our relationships with others.

7

Enhancing Relationship

Voice Dialogue

We have used many different methods and approaches to deepen the relationship between us and to enhance our own personal process. Each technique, each new approach to consciousness or personal growth, contributes something important of its own, but without question, Voice Dialogue has been our favorite. It works the best for us, and it has been the most fun to use.

We are aware, of course, that we just might be a little bit prejudiced, because Voice Dialogue is a child of our relationship. It was born of our love and of our work together, and its theoretical base developed out of our own need to keep our relationship alive and vital. Our book, *Embracing Our Selves*, is essentially a training manual that describes the use of Voice Dialogue in detail.

Although one usually requires some training to learn how to use Voice Dialogue and to become an effective facilitator, some therapists and people of considerable experience with consciousness work have reported to us that they actually started to use the method successfully after reading the manual. It is impossible for us to do justice to this method of working with one's selves in this book, so all we can do is to recommend that the reader consult *Embracing Our Selves* or make arrangements to experience Voice Dialogue with a facilitator who has already been trained in the work.

The Voice Dialogue process involves working directly with one's various selves. It is deceptively simple and surprisingly powerful. It can be especially helpful to use in relationship, because it gives people the opportunity to communicate safely with one another's selves. When Voice Dialogue is used in relationship, it enables individuals to have direct experience of, and to broaden their understanding of, their own selves, the selves in other people, and of the bonding patterns that seem to run their lives. Needless to say, this promotes intense intimacy and a most thorough understanding of one another and of one another's process. However, as in any kind of exploration, one does not know exactly what might come up. Reading our book and receiving training from a therapist and/or teacher who does Voice Dialogue training is what we would recommend for anyone who is interested in learning about this process. Even though you might not actually be able to practice Voice Dialogue, you can use your understanding of selves to greatly enhance the communication process between yourself and others.

Let us say that Barbara and Norman have gone to a party. Barbara is feeling somewhat withdrawn afterwards, and Norman asks her what is wrong. She says that nothing is wrong. Norman senses her withdrawal and, utilizing his understanding of subpersonalities, asks her how her little girl is doing. With this, she bursts into tears and all of her feelings of vulnerability and inadequacy come pouring out. Without the knowledge that there is a vulnerable child within each of us, Norman might have simply been put off by Barbara's withdrawal. His own feelings could have been hurt, and the two of them would have been off and running toward a bonding pattern where blame and recrimination ruled the communication.

Jean and Bob go to a movie and Bob feels very depressed afterwards. He has a hard time expressing his feelings. If Jean was to ask him what he was feeling, little would be expressed, because he really doesn't know. However, if she was aware of the selves, she could ask Bob to get in touch with them and see how each of them feels.

The theme of the film was the portrayal of a man who was dying of cancer. Jean asks Bob if he can get in touch with the part of himself that is afraid of dying. He is able to do this, and it is as though he is able to speak from this place. Then he realizes that it is not dying that he fears, but rather being crippled or mutilated, being unable to function physically.

Jean then asks Bob whether there is a part of him that is specifically afraid of cancer. He is shocked at this but soon is able to get in touch with the part of him that has always been terrified of getting cancer. Several members of his family have died of cancer, and he, or a part of him, has had this fear from the time he was twenty, when his mother died.

It is very often a deep relief to realize that there are different parts of us, that these different parts feel and think quite differently about things, and that this is perfectly normal and natural. We will see other examples of this kind of communication in this chapter.

Letting Go

Most of us are strongly motivated to protect our relationships at any cost. Once our dominant selves, whoever they may be, feel that they have found a safe harbor, they want us to stay put. They are not about to start out again on new journeys in unfamiliar waters. Perhaps the most difficult part of any relationship, and certainly one of the most difficult aspects of our own relationship, has been the process of letting go of each other over and over again.

We have found that as soon as we become attached to being together for the rest of our lives, the primary selves take over and begin to limit our possibilities. When we let go, accept the possibility that our relationship cannot be controlled and that there well may be surprises ahead, we are able to communicate more freely and completely. We move into a position where we can receive input from selves other than the primary ones. Our awareness is expanded, and our consciousness includes far more information than it can possibly receive from just our primary selves. At this point we can notice possibilities that had not existed before, our lives become more spontaneous and our solutions to problems more creative.

In our own relationship, we fully expect to remain together. After all that we have been through, it seems highly unlikely that a separation would occur. Yet we are also open to the possibility that the process of our relationship could lead us in another direction. It is not what either of us would want at this point, but we profoundly respect the process of our relationship, how it has been our teacher, and how it is always possible for it to take us in an entirely different direction than is our conscious intent at this point.

This is a painful idea for many people. When they get married, they want it to be forever. *Of one thing, however, we may be sure: there are no insurance policies when it comes to primary relationship. There is only process.* When an insurance policy is obtained, we can be fairly certain that a strong pattern of bonding will emerge in the relationship. *The price we pay for total security and well-being in relationship is, generally speaking, an increasing loss of vitality, romance, sexuality, and general creativity in the relationship.* This is not always the case, but we have seen it happen with considerable frequency.

Because we basically feel that one needs to hold a relationship with great care, but in an open hand, this chapter is not intended as a guide for making any specific relationship work. If one follows the path of relationship, if one truly surrenders to the process of relationship rather than to the other person, then the relationship will take both partners forward to the next stage in their evolution of consciousness. This may mean that they will be together or it may mean that they will move apart. Whichever it means, the process will be a natural one that grows inevitably out of the deepest needs of the two partners. This does not mean that there may not be regret, sadness, or even great pain if a primary relationship must end, but it does mean that the participants will gain in wisdom and they will move forward in their personal evolution of consciousness as they move on from each relationship that they have known.

Sometimes it takes many years for those involved to appreciate the gifts that a particular relationship has conferred, but each has, in fact, given them something. Not all relationships are supposed to last. A relationship that may be appropriate for one period of our lives may not necessarily be appropriate for another. It is important to trust that this works both ways; *either a relationship is good for both partners, or it is good for neither.*

Sometimes the relationship must actually break or time must pass after the break before this becomes apparent. For instance, Sam had been married to Joan for five years, but he was very unhappy. Joan, in turn, was severely depressed. She had even required hospitalization from time to time. They lived a deeply bonded relationship, with his responsible father bonded to her disturbed daughter. Sam, in the responsible father, felt that he could not leave Joan because he was afraid that she might commit suicide. It appeared to everyone that Sam was sacrificing his life for Joan and that she needed him desperately. Finally, with great trepidation, and at a time when Joan was safely hospitalized, Sam asked for a divorce.

Surprisingly, enough, Joan recovered from her depression immediately, left the hospital, lost the weight that she had gained during their years of marriage, and resumed a normal life. The bonded marriage had been costing her as much as it had cost him.

A relationship that must end at one time in life because of the current level of consciousness may well be appropriate at some later time. Edith and Arnie loved each other passionately in high school, but Edith felt that Arnie would not make a good husband. She wanted someone more sophisticated, a man whom she could look up to and admire, not someone she felt was her equal, like Arnie.

Edith's inadequate daughter sought out a strong man to bond to her as a knowing, sophisticated father. She married John instead of Arnie because she was fascinated by his intelligence and sophistication.

As the years rolled by, Edith lived a life of elegance and sophistication. She integrated her own sophisticated lady and became quite comfortable with her own knowledge. She was no longer the ardent admirer of John's apparent wisdom. They slowly drifted apart. It was the bonding of her daughter and his sophisticated father that had pulled them together in the first place. When this dissipated, there was nothing left to attract them to one another. They divorced.

Some time after the divorce, Arnie heard that Edith was free again, he contacted her, and they resumed the intense love relationship that had been theirs in the early years. Only this time it was a mature relationship of two aware egos, and this time it ended in a happy marriage that was a great source of comfort to both of them.

Trying too hard to make a specific relationship work at any particular time, rather than trusting that it will work if it is appropriate, can be damaging to all concerned. When any of us is too attached to a particular relationship, too worried about losing it, then we are often willing to perform all kinds of psychological self-mutilation to ensure its continuation. If, on the other hand, we surrender to the process of relationship, we can trust that if we are fully ourselves, an appropriate relationship will prosper and an inappropriate one will end in a natural fashion.

Personal Sharing

Personal sharing is a prerequisite for a relationship that is dedicated to growth and the evolution of consciousness. Facing facts is hard work, but it is important. It is only through an honest confrontation of what is happening in a relationship that deep contact is maintained and that growth occurs.

Generally speaking, the more openness we can bring to a relationship, the better off we are. Holding back feelings and reactions usually has the effect of creating more and more distance between partners.

Sharing feelings, however, is frequently easier said than done. The feelings may be out of our sphere of awareness or they may simply produce too much pain, or the possibility of too much pain, if we try to communicate them. It is also important to be aware of how the inner critic attacks us very often when we cannot share our feelings. If we cannot share them, we simply need to be aware that they are there, that we cannot allow them expression now, and we must not allow ourselves to be criticized because we are unable to express them. We must know that at the right time they will be ready to emerge.

Much of what we feel at any given moment of time is unconscious. All forms of psychological work are valuable, because they help us to learn more and more about the things that are going on inside of ourselves. We have already described how it is possible to share feelings more easily if we are aware of the many different parts of ourselves and how they might be feeling in a particular situation.

If we were to ask you how you were feeling at this particular moment, you might not have too much to say. Imagine that we said the following to you: "We would like to know how the different parts of you are feeling and thinking right now while you are reading this book. How does your intellectual self feel? Your objective scientist? Your intuitive self? Your vulnerable child? Your responsible father/mother and husband/wife? Your free spirit? Your sexual psychopath?"

These different selves would give very different answers, assuming it were possible for you to experience them at some level and tune in to their feelings and thoughts. What interesting conversations we humans would have, how multidimensional would be our communications, if we were able to bring to each other the fullness and richness of these many selves.

There is also a danger in the sharing process. This danger is seen particularly in people who have come from backgrounds where extensive personal growth work has taken place. What we see with considerable frequency is a compulsive requirement to always be talking and processing, no matter how the other person feels about it. In this kind of situation, there is no respect for introversion or privacy, and the people are not communicating from an aware ego.

When you are able to share personally from an aware ego, you find that you are in touch with the fear of your frightened child, the empathy that your vulnerable child feels for the other, and the cool clarity of your impersonal self, which can face facts just as they are and present them in a straightforward fashion. You will have an awareness available to you that can look at the entire situation dispassionately and feed you the information that you need from moment to moment. This allows both the other person and you to react in a non-bonded fashion from an aware ego. You are both free to examine whatever is happening without trying to control the course of the conversation.

It is amazing how many times a seemingly selfish request, or a fantasy, or an apparently unfounded reaction will open up new vistas in a relationship or trigger a new step in the evolution of your consciousness. Roger is dismayed to find that he is no longer sexually attracted to Veronica, his wife. He has not told her this because, in his responsible father, he did not want to hurt her feelings, and he sees that she does everything in her power to be attractive to him. He knows about relationship as a teacher, however, and he decides to take the chance and share this reaction with her.

As Roger expresses his concern in a way that incorporates both his power and his vulnerability, he is surprised to learn that Veronica has been aware of this decreasing interest and that she, too, has felt a lessening of sexual desire for him. She, too, is unhappy about this, because she loves him very much. Her frightened child had not wanted to hear what was wrong and her responsible mother did not want to hurt him, so she had not said anything about this matter herself.

They continue on, allowing themselves to express any reactions that come to the surface. As the conversation progresses, they discover that Roger has gradually, over the past two years, given up his contacts with his men friends. He used to have many friends and had enjoyed meeting them for dinner, but he began to feel that Veronica would be happier if he remained home at night. Without either of them being aware of what was happening, he had given up his meetings with his friends.

As Roger becomes aware of how important his friends are and starts making plans to see them again, Veronica suddenly remembers that she had planned to begin graduate school when their youngest child entered kindergarten. The youngest child is already in third grade and Veronica is still spending her entire life in the responsible mother role, caring for everyone and not beginning to pursue a career of her own. Both Roger and Veronica are delighted to find that their needs mesh. This is so often the case, if we pursue our personal sharing to the very end.

Veronica and Roger make plans that on Thursday nights he will have dinner with his friends, she will go to school, and the children will visit with the grandparents, who have been asking to see more of them. Thus, the parent/child bonding between Roger and Veronica is cut into for the moment, and new vistas open up for each of them. Neither is hurt or feels abandoned (as the responsible parent selves had feared), and both are excited by their new plans. Their sexuality returns automatically to the relationship. Sexuality usually returns to its former level of intensity in a relationship when a bonding pattern is broken and the next step forward has been taken.

Personal sharing does not deal with emotional reactions alone. This kind of sharing includes sharing in all areas of life. How many of us have thought at one time or another in our lives, "It's fine that I'm loved now when I'm behaving appropriately, but what if they knew what I'm really like underneath?" We have all been raised to hide as much of ourselves, or, shall we say, as many of our selves, as are necessary in order to gain love and acceptance.

It is in our relationships that we have the chance to open ourselves up to other people. Often in marriage, people are unable and/or unwilling to show the fullness of themselves to each other when they are quite able to show these parts of themselves to a friend. This is a sure mark of a bonding pattern in the marriage relationship and an indication of potential trouble ahead.

Needless to say, most of us are usually not shy about personal sharing in areas that feel comfortable to us. Some areas, however, are more problematical. Others are areas we may never have thought about sharing with someone else.

Two topics that are frequently uncomfortable are our concerns about our money and our health. There is often a good deal of fear or vulnerability associated with both of these areas. As we have seen previously, a worried vulnerable child invariably precipitates a bonding pattern if it is ignored. Our vulnerable children have a habit of worrying about our aches and pains and about our financial stability. Therefore, if there is concern in either area, it is important to open it up for discussion.

The refusal to share one's concerns in these areas of vulnerability almost invariably causes bonding patterns to develop. We have found that joint consideration of financial and health matters gives much comfort in most relationships and helps to promote consciousness and far better decision making when both partners have input in these areas. After all, both people will be deeply affected by whatever happens.

There is another area of difficulty so far as sharing is concerned, and that concerns something physical that bothers us about our partner. This might be a partner's weight, the way she dresses, the fact that he is losing his hair. This is a particularly sensitive area, because if these kinds of feelings are not shared, they tend to grow out of all proportion.

The issue once again has to do with what part of us gives the reaction. An attacking father can be very destructive in a situation like this. An aware ego will be in touch with vulnerability, and it will come through very differently.

Last but not least is the sharing of fantasies. Most of us are not trained to share our fantasies except, perhaps, with our therapists. Sharing fantasies, however, allows us to know one another at an entirely new level of intimacy.

We have already looked at the sharing of sexual attractions or fantasies about other people in our discussion of attractions and affairs. This is likely to lead to new growth in a relationship. It can also be used with great fun in actual sexual activities. Many people enjoy playing out their sexual fantasies with one another, enriching their sexual encounters and adding to their variety.

For most couples it is difficult to share fantasies, for they are often the core of our disowned selves. They represent our most private spaces, our deepest secrets, our greatest shame. To be able to open these parts of ourselves in a relationship is an act of great intimacy and courage. This is an important part of who we are. What better place to show this side of ourselves than in an intimate relationship? We say this knowing full well how much the protector/controller may not want this to happen. *We must, however, repeat our basic injunction that the feelings of the protector/controller must be honored in whatever we do and say.*

In general, the point of sharing fantasies is to make us feel closer to each other. Sometimes, when we share a fantasy with our partner, it plants a psychic seed that grows into reality. One never can tell what will happen once one's fantasy is spoken out loud to a lover.

Dealing with Negativity in Relationship

Most of us find that sharing our negative reactions with one another is even more difficult than generalized personal sharing of our process and feelings. Our vulnerable child is afraid of abandonment, our critic tells us that we are making mountains out of molehills, our pleaser tells us that we have to be nice to people or they will not love us, our nurturing parent tells us that our partner is unable to bear the pain that our negativity will cause, and our protector/controller most probably will warn us that we are risking the relationship. In addition to all this, we love our partner and, even in an aware ego, we do not want to inflict any pain.

Unless we are in our judgmental parent and fully self-righteous, most of us will not look forward to this part of a relationship. But unfortunately, if we bury enough negative reactions, they have a tendency to build up and threaten the relationship. Those negative dragons have a way of growing extra heads very quickly when they are not dealt with appropriately.

There is a point in all relationships when the "falling in love" phase is over and we look at one another more soberly. Small annoyances begin to crop up. We suddenly realize that our partner does not close the kitchen cupboards after opening them or turn off the lights when leaving a room. Clothes are left lying around. Or, conversely, our partner is too neat and demands that we straighten up the house each day. One of us likes the window open, the other likes it closed. In the interest of peace, we withhold our reactions. At some point, however, we must say something, or all our energy will be spent holding back reactions, and the spontaneity, vitality, and sexuality will disappear from the relationship.

Surprisingly enough, when negative reactions are shared through an aware ego, there is usually less discomfort than most of us might imagine. When we are sharing our reactions through an aware ego, there is no judgment and no blame. This makes it far more likely that our partner will be receptive to what we have to say.

Negative reactions—even negative reactions that are expressed through one of our power selves—are not to be judged. It is simply a question of becoming aware at some point of where they came from. *Learning to spend more time in the aware ego, and to express our negative reactions through the aware ego, becomes one of the working goals of relationship.* In a relationship that involves all of our selves, our partner is usually already aware of these negative reactions at some level. They have been transmitted in non-verbal form, energetically through body language, through our unconscious acts, our slips of the tongue or even through our jokes; therefore, they are rarely a total surprise.

Actually, the denial of these reactions has served to distance us from one another. In most instances talking things out helps to bring us back together with our partner, and, quite frequently, creative solutions can be reached that can deal effectively with many of our irritations.

Negative reactions, when brought through an aware ego, can also break bonding patterns. If both partners are in their aware egos, they are facing facts, and it is quite possible to learn from one another through these negative reactions. For example, there may be times when one or the other partner in a relationship becomes too identified with the perfectionist, too much at the mercy of a critic, too frequently the rescuing parent, or too dominated by the pusher. A clear reaction by the other may help to break the hold of that particular self and allow in something new.

Negative reactions, clearly presented, often signal the time for a change in consciousness. Relationships, when

consciously lived, demand a great deal of all of us. When it is
time to move on, to try something new, or to give up an old
and no longer useful way of being in life, our partner's
negative reaction may well be the catalyst.

Upon close examination, we all find that our *intensely*
judgmental negative reactions to our partners are a reflection
of our own disowned selves. You have seen numerous examples of this in previous chapters. In a relationship that
encourages the exploration of these negative reactions, you
are therefore quite likely to be brought face to face with your
disowned selves. Working with your partner in this way can
give you an unparalleled opportunity to find out about these
selves and embrace them.

This is another way that you can truly get the most out of
relationship. If you do not remain open to the possibility that
a negative and judgmental reaction is a sign that a disowned
self has been activated within you, then you not only lose an
opportunity to continue your own personal growth, but you
also may lock into a particularly unpleasant bonding pattern
with your partner. Your partner will then become more and
more entrenched in the self that you disown, as you become
more and more entrenched in its opposite. You may become
more and more responsible as your partner becomes less and
less so; you may become more disorganized and your partner
more in control. This makes for great comedy, as anyone
who has seen *The Odd Couple* knows, but it is not much fun in
a primary relationship.

Sexuality

Sexuality is a major part of life and an extremely important
aspect of a primary love relationship. The contributions that
an active sexual involvement can make to the physical,
emotional, mental, and spiritual well-being of an individual

can hardly be overestimated. Therefore, taking care to do whatever it is that promotes this aspect of relationship is important.

This will be different for different people. For some it may mean paying more attention to one's physical body. For others, it may mean consciously setting aside adequate time and taking care to arrange for an appropriate romantic setting. For still others, it may mean gathering new information on sexuality in its many forms and allowing themselves the freedom to experiment. There are even those for whom a fulfilling sexual relationship comes quite naturally, people who instinctively treasure and protect the sexual aspects of relationship. Whatever one does, however, it would seem that this aspect of one's relationship should be properly honored. As we have said on many occasions, Aphrodite, the goddess of love, is not a goddess to ignore.

In the day-to-day experience of relationship, we have found that sexuality is directly affected by the quality of the emotional contact between the two partners. It is usually pretty difficult to achieve a fulfilling sexual relationship when the relationship itself is dominated by bonding patterns. We have seen this in our own relationship and we have seen this in others'. Needless to say, we find that this loss of sexuality gives us all the more motivation to work our way out of bonding patterns when they begin to form.

Over the years, we have found that one of the best guardians of the sexual relationship is an aware ego. A young woman had been away from her boyfriend for a month on a vacation trip that she took alone. When she returned, she identified with her strong academic pusher and began her semester at school. Her boyfriend, a sensitive man, was very unhappy and told her that she was not present. She was quite annoyed with him and by this time had no feeling for him at all.

In a conversation, a friend pointed out she had disappeared, that her academic pusher had taken over her life. Her aware ego suddenly re-emerged as she separated from her pusher side and with amazement she remarked: "I forgot how attracted I am to him!"

Young parents often enter into the bonding pattern of responsible father and responsible mother. This is very natural in the early stages of marriage, and it is always present to some extent when there are young children in the home.

As they fall further and further into the responsible parent roles, couples find themselves less and less interested in sex. Somehow, one of them is always busy or tired. There are other, seemingly more important, things to think about: there is the problem of arranging for good child care and driving carpools, making sure that the children are getting the most out of life, their plans for the new house, the people at work who depend upon them, the friends who need them, their aging parents who require more attention each year. They love each other dearly, but, to their disappointment, they begin to think of themselves as a great team with much to accomplish, rather than as lovers. And a great team they are, but they have lost the most precious part of their relationship in all this attention to the demands of daily living. It takes real commitment to move out of this type of bonding.

Veronica and Roger, in the example given earlier, show this commitment. They want to maintain the vitality of their relationship, and they work with each other until they break their bonding. They are able to do this themselves, but many people need outside help to do this.

When Roger and Veronica's bonding is broken, and each of them moves out of the responsible parent role, their sexuality returns to their relationship. In this new consciousness, they automatically both give romance a high priority and, somehow, find the time for it. They are able to do all this and be responsible parents to their children as well. It requires creativity, but, as we have said, they are a great team.

Another bonding pattern typically occurs later in life.

Herbert is vulnerable and anxious about his health and about his age, and he gradually moves into his vulnerable child/ withdrawn father. This, of course, destroys the sexual relationship completely. He will not even approach his wife, Dinah, and if she were to approach him, he would withdraw. Moreover, his movement into the withdrawn father has pushed her into the needy daughter, and the sexual advances of the needy daughter are usually not too attractive.

This is a particularly pernicious bonding, because as the sexuality becomes less attractive to both Herbert and Dinah, he feels even older, more fearful, and more vulnerable, and withdraws further into his withdrawn father. This intensifies the bonding and the emotional distance between them.

It is precisely this kind of bonding that can lead to a premature cessation of sexual activity in a primary relationship. Sex then becomes a topic to be avoided at all costs, and the decline in sexuality is seen as a natural concomitant to the aging process. The loss of sexuality has intensified the bonding and the bonding has resulted in the erosion of sexuality.

Sometimes, however, we have found an active sexual involvement in a deeply bonded relationship. With the current emphasis upon good sexuality, we have seen a surprising amount of sexuality these days that is the bonded sexuality of responsible parent to needy child.

The responsible parent is not a very sexual self and brings little excitement and depth to the sexual experience. However, a responsible parent knows that sex is important for her child's well-being, and many a responsible mother has made sure that her husband's needy son gets his necessary share of sexual satisfaction. She may even keep an informal calendar in her head, knowing how many days have elapsed since the last sexual interchange.

This is usually better than nothing, but it is not too great. Think of having someone make love to you for essentially the same reason that she makes peanut butter and jelly sandwiches for the children.

When this kind of bonded sexuality persists, both partners are usually dissatisfied, but it is difficult for them to
figure out what is wrong. They may have frequent sexual
contact; they may even both experience orgasm on a regular
basis. Nothing seems to be wrong, but still, there is something missing. This is one of the bonding patterns that can be
brought to one's attention, as it was to Veronica and Roger's,
by personal sharing.

Another frequent type of bonded sexuality is the demanding father/compliant daughter. This is the more classical sexual bonding pattern that we have seen in the past. In
this, the woman submits to sex because it is demanded of
her. She may even enjoy it from time to time, but it does not
emerge from her own sexual nature and she is not involved in
the same way as she would be if it had. Since sexual activity is
not her responsibility, she never gets to experience the
delight of her own desire or the power of her own needs. We
are not talking here of the physical coercion to have sexual
relations, we are just talking of the daily ordinary bonded
pressure from the demanding father in the man. The pressure from the demanding father often comes about because
the man disowns his vulnerability and neediness. He has a
physical need that makes him vulnerable and he has an
emotional need as well. He wants to be wanted. If the woman
in his life does not respond to him with her own sexuality, he
often feels sexually inadequate and emotionally vulnerable,
and as he disowns this, he is quite likely to move into the role
of demanding father.

The bonding of the controlling sexual mother/depend-
ent son can be extremely powerful. In this, the woman uses
her sexuality to protect her disowned vulnerability and to
control the man. Rather than disown her sexuality as the
compliant daughter, she enhances it and uses it in the service
of power. As the controlling mother she does everything
possible to seduce him and to make him dependent upon her.
She may deliberately make herself available to him at all
times, in the hope of keeping him monogamous and thereby

protecting her vulnerability. She keeps the sexual contacts intense and exciting, sometimes more in an effort to control him and keep him dependent than as an expression of her own sexuality.

The more she emphasizes her own intense sexuality, and the more she enhances the sexual contact, the more she may intensify his fear of sexual inadequacy and his dependence upon her more passionate sexuality. There are many role models for her in our pop culture.

We feel that certain cultural attitudes toward sexuality tend to fuel bonding patterns. We are pushed by these societal attitudes to assume either a child or parent position.

Let us see how this works. There is much in advertising and the media that deliberately stimulates the vulnerable child in each of us in regard to our own sexual attractiveness or adequacy. We are constantly bombarded with images of astoundingly sexual or superbly attractive people and encouraged to emulate them. We are told how many orgasms we should have and what intensity they should reach. We are shown pictures of the most beautiful, glamorous, superbly dressed men and women. We are brought face to face with our own inadequacies repeatedly.

We cannot possibly measure up to these images, because they are not real. James Bond is a fictitious character. Most men are not, and never will be, James Bond. Nor, upon serious consideration, would most women want them to be.

Expectations of women's sexuality are so pervasive that it is difficult to single out one example that is as obvious for them as James Bond is for men. Women are constantly being reminded of how much sexier they should be and told what they can do about it. There is almost no respite from this pressure.

When these expectations of super-sexuality are set up in the general consciousness, as we have seen, they activate the vulnerable child or the inadequate child within. Most men do not measure up if they choose to compare themselves to James Bond. Most women cannot meet the demands placed upon them by *Cosmopolitan* magazine. Even if these are not our personal ideals, they represent major idealized images in our predominant culture. Since nobody likes to remain sexually inadequate and suffer the kind of discomfort that is caused by not measuring up to these ideals, there is a tendency to move over to the power side and exaggerate one's prowess by identifying with a kind of sexual superhero, thus escalating the entire bonding process. In a more extreme form of this bonding, one becomes identified with sexual power and uses it quite deliberately to control others. This power has been traditionally used by women who, in our culture, had few alternative ways in which to wield real power in the world in the past. One of the classic heroines, Scarlett O'Hara, gives the most striking example of this use of the power of sexuality, particularly when all else seems lost and she is totally vulnerable.

Men, when feeling vulnerable, often move into a more aggressive or even violent sexuality as a way to dominate others and to prove their superiority. When this movement is extreme, it can take a man from intense vulnerability to exaggerated sexual power in the form of sadism. This has led many feminist writers to feel that there has been a serious confusion of sexuality and violence in our culture.

These bonding patterns bring great difficulty and confusion into one of the most exciting, rewarding, intimacy-enhancing aspects of relationship. The gifts brought by a simple and naturally functioning sexual relationship are so great that the loss of this part of a relationship often motivates movement forward, just so that the sexuality will return once again. This return of one's presumably lost sexual feelings after a bonding pattern has been broken is an awe-inspiring experience that brings with it great physical release and, needless to say, a tremendous sigh of relief.

Jealousy

A short word on jealousy, a most maligned aspect of relationship. There are many kinds of jealousy and there are many causes, but jealousy, when appropriate and moderate, does much to support a primary relationship.

There has been a strong tendency in recent years to view jealousy as something bad. There is no way of being or feeling or thinking that is essentially bad or good. It is always a question of how the energy is used. Since we love one another and we want to guard our relationship from erosion, we are both quite sensitive to anyone or anything that could conceivably cause damage to it. *We look upon normal jealousy as a protective mechanism. It is like pain. Pain warns us that there is something wrong.* If you did not feel pain, you would not know when one of your feet was in a campfire and that you should remove it.

There is no great advantage not to feel the pain. As a matter of fact, people who do not feel pain can get very badly hurt. Your foot, for instance, could remain in the campfire until you smelled burned flesh, if you were unfortunate enough to have a problem with the pain receptors in that particular foot.

Jealousy can alert us to problems in our relationship. If we are caught in a bonding pattern and one of us is attracted to someone else, our jealous reaction alerts us to this, perhaps even before the attracted partner is actually aware of the attraction. The jealous partner is then in a position to bring the matter into awareness. After the first blood is drawn, we can open the issue to a creative process and see our parts in the dance of the selves that led up to this. We have found that growth inevitably follows an exploration of selves that has been initiated by a jealous reaction.

There is one other creative aspect of jealousy that should be noted. *Jealousy is a powerful indicator of a disowned self.* If you see someone as more attractive, more sophisticated, more powerful, more wise, more creative, more spiritual, more self-indulgent, or any of the myriad other "mores" that can be brought to mind, and you are jealous, you are probably looking at a disowned self. This can lead to the exploration and integration of a new, and usually a very welcome, disowned self. This disowned self is one that you wanted but thought belonged only to others, rather than a disowned self that you had found distasteful in others and had not wanted for your own.

Jack is jealous of his brother Bob, because Bob is very wealthy and quite successful in his investments and business dealings. At a certain point in Jack's life, he discovers that the whole world of business and finance is a disowned self of his, and he begins to honor it and embrace this part of himself. He never is going to have as much money as his brother has, but as he begins to honor the world of business and finance, as he gets this part of his life organized, his feelings of jealousy dissipate to a large extent. He has embraced a disowned self, and so he no longer has to be intensely jealous of people who are identified with their business selves and who are successful in the world of finance.

A different kind of example would be that of Nan. She feels very jealous of her husband, and she is somewhat ashamed of the fact. She has mentioned on a number of occasions that she is jealous of him when she sees him with other women at the parties they attend. He is quick to reassure her that it is all quite innocent. She then dreams for three nights running that he is having an affair. When she finally confronts him in the morning after the third of these dreams, he admits to the affair and to others besides this one. Her jealousy was quite justified and had given her some very important information.

Alice is very much identified with her vulnerability and frequently feels like a victim. She disowns her own Aphrodite energy, and so she is very jealous of her husband's secretary, who is an Aphrodite type. One must learn to take jealousy seriously, but one must also learn to examine the possibility that one's disowned selves are involved in the matter. Alice remained jealous of her husband and brought up her suspicions over and over again, accusing him of an involvement with his secretary. Eventually, her husband did enter into a relationship with the secretary, which ultimately broke up the marriage.

In our view, the inability of Alice to face her own Aphrodite nature, and to integrate it, literally created the fate that she so much feared. Her disowning of the Aphrodite energy within herself had created an energetic vacuum in the relationship with her husband. It may have happened under any circumstances, but our own experience and viewpoint are that things would have turned out differently had she been able to come to grips with her jealousy and understand the lessons it was trying to teach her.

Marriage as a Business Relationship

Life is very complicated. There are myriads of details that seem to increase as the years roll along. Each day has its own list of chores and activities and plans and planning and carpools and house cleaning and gardening and bills to be paid and calls to be made and cars to be repaired and purchases to be investigated and shopping to be done. It is always amazing how much there is to do in what seems should be the rather simple business of running a modern household.

The vulnerable child within is generally very anxious about the world, and it is very important from the child's standpoint that the details of living are taken care of properly; otherwise there is a great deal of anxiety. What this means in family relationships is that the couple, in addition to everything else that they are doing, are running a business and are business partners. *Being good business partners is not necessarily conducive to the maintenance of a romantic relationship. Not being good business partners and allowing the details of life to be ignored is guaranteed to be destructive to relationship.*

If we accept marriage as, in part, a business relationship, then we have to honor this by providing time for the business to be transacted. Otherwise, the business enters into every facet of one's life. We personally feel it is very valuable to have regular business meetings. At these times, we talk over everything that has to be done, establish priorities, and then decide who is to do what. We find that it is extremely valuable for us to give the business side of our relationship this kind of structure, particularly because our professional and our personal lives are intermingled. It helps very much in containing the business side of the relationship and not allowing it to spill over into the rest of our lives. It also helps us in the containing of pusher energy by providing a structure as to what needs to be done.

What we are all struggling with is the issue of maximizing the amount of intimacy we can have in our relationships. Too much attention being paid to business can destroy intimacy. Too little attention being paid to business can destroy intimacy through the anxiety that is created. It is a difficult balance that each of us must wrestle with in our lives.

Leaving the Known Place

There is a meditation that is used to help people get in touch with their deeper selves. It begins with the statement: "You are leaving the known space of this room and going into a new space that is unknown to you."

This introduction to meditation is very appropriate when we think about couples living together in a home or an apartment, especially when there are children involved. It seems to us of the utmost importance for couples to leave their known space and move into an unknown space, or more practically, a different space.

What this means is that we feel it is essential for couples to leave their regular place of living and to spend time somewhere else. It is best if this can be an overnight somewhere, or even a few nights. Short of this, it might mean a regular dinner out once a week or a breakfast out once a week. *Wherever you live on an ongoing basis, your basic bonding patterns are operating. When you leave home, you have the chance of separating from these patterns.*

This is different from going away with the children. When children are around, the father and mother selves are active. Alone, you have the chance to have a different kind of experience. The aware ego has a better chance to emerge, and you have an opportunity of seeing one another in a new light and new way.

There are always good reasons for not getting away. There is not enough money or not enough time. There is a party to go to or the children need you. *When you stop making time to be alone, you are locked into a bonding pattern, and it is the bonding pattern that makes it impossible to get away, not all the reasons you can muster. Intimacy with another human being requires time alone with that person. It must be given priority and needs to be built into the system on some regular basis.* When finances are an issue, arrangements can be made with other couples with similar needs to take turns taking care of one another's children.

The "Being" State and Silent Time

One of the extraordinary things about primary relationship is how little time people spend together in silence. Talking is fun, but it can also be one of the most effective ways there is of destroying intimacy. Most of us are identified with an action and doing principle. The doing self always needs to be doing something. With another person, this would refer to talking or participating in some activity together. The opposite side of the doing self is the being self. In "being" energy, there is nothing to do except "be." There is no place to go, nothing to plan, nothing to accomplish. There is nothingness, a void, and many people are quite terrified of this condition. To "be" with another human being means just what it says. It means to be with someone with no agenda of any kind. There are often long periods of silence, or words may come, but they come from a different place in ourselves because there is no requirement that they come at all.

This condition of "beingness" can be painful for people because it is a condition of deep intimacy, and they feel really uncomfortable about this kind of closeness. What we recommend is taking time to practice "being" together. This means just sitting together on a couch or two chairs and just looking at one another and allowing there to be silence. Getting used to silence can profoundly change the nature of relationship. The reason for this is that in silence you tend to come to a more essential part of yourself. While in a "being" state it is natural for all kinds of thoughts and feelings to come up. Just share them with each other. It creates a kind of flow of association, a non-linear thought flow that is much fun and very relaxing, once you learn to get into it and move through the initial period of discomfort and even anxiety.

It is natural in relationships of all kinds to react immediately when someone reacts to you. There is almost an automatic response of "yes, but. . ." These kinds of automatic responses do not allow you to take in fully the reactions of the other person. The being self allows you to receive the feelings and reactions of the other person without needing to automatically and immediately respond to them.

Sometimes we recommend to couples that they take turns practicing "active listening." This means that if there are issues in the relationship, one person shares while the other person is silent but actively listening to what is being said until there is nothing else to say. Then, after yet a further period of silence, they reverse roles. In this way, couples can train themselves to live with silence and to better receive the feelings of the other person.

Words are connected to our more established patterns of thought and behavior and feeling. Silence opens us to the deeper aspects of ourselves. *In silence we feel our vulnerability, our tears, our sadness, our soul. To be together in silence is to create the possibility of a much more profound experience of intimacy.*

Visual Imagery in Relationship

A great gift that can be given in relationship is the experience of direct inner exploration. This can be accomplished by leading one's partner in active imagination or visual imagery.

The technique is a simple one. One partner is the subject and the other the guide. A quiet space is chosen and arrangements are made so that there will be no interruptions or distractions.

The subject assumes a comfortable position, usually lying down and, if necessary, covered with a blanket. The subject's eyes are closed or covered with a mask so that there will be no visual distractions. The partner who is facilitating then begins to lead the visualization.

First, there is the suggestion to relax and breathe deeply. Then, the actual journey begins. The point of departure can be left open completely, and the subject can look for whatever image might emerge. A particularly haunting dream can be re-entered and the action picked up from where it left off. The partners can agree beforehand that there will be a particular path followed. One may suggest that the subject is going to some new kind of place that exists only in his or her own imagination. It might be a meadow or a forest or mountain, or beach, or it might even mean leaving the planet.

There are all kinds of possibilities. Visualization can take many different forms and contains all kinds of surprises for the explorers of the psyche. We are entering here into the realm of the creative imagination. Sometimes the journey opens up entirely new areas of imagery. For others who do not visualize, different thought forms can emerge—new ideas, stories, fairy tales, untold possibilities.

On these journeys we meet different kinds of people, animals, symbols, and energies of all kinds. It is often possible to talk with these different figures, to learn from them, but with an aware ego that can evaluate the material that is being experienced. These inner journeys can be extremely enriching and often bring much light to bear on the relationship. They can give a picture of the relationship as it is, and they can give guidance on where it is going or what needs to be done.

The development of wisdom and the acceleration of the evolution of consciousness can be directly supported in relationship by regular use of visualization. In this way, we can help one another gain access to inner knowledge by leading our partners, or friends, in these visualizations.

There are many books on guided imagery and many excellent teachers. One that we strongly recommend is called *Creative Visualization*, written by Shakti Gawain and published by New World Library in San Rafael, California. There is also an extensive literature in psychosynthesis to help us in these explorations. If this type of work appeals to a couple, they can study together and make this kind of exploration an ongoing process, which can add an unbelievably rich dimension to the relationship.

Ritual and Spiritual Practices in Relationship

We feel that the inclusion of some kind of ritual or spiritual practice is another important aspect of relationship. These activities are quite personal in nature and will vary greatly from couple to couple. For some, membership in a religious or spiritual organization and taking time to follow the specific practices of this group will work beautifully.

These organizations provide ritual observances that serve a variety of spiritual needs. Going to the church of one's choice, saying a blessing over one's food, and keeping the Sabbath are observances that have withstood the test of time. When they are followed wholeheartedly, they bring many couples the truly rewarding spiritual experience they seek.

Other couples find their needs served by spiritual organizations that have their roots in Eastern religions or in the Native American beliefs and ritual observances. Many people have developed their own spiritual practices.

Some couples find that daily meditation together fulfills their needs for joint spiritual activity. Others take time for prayers at a regular time such as at meals, in the morning upon rising, or in the evening before retiring. Other couples may join groups that come together to observe particular holidays, not in a traditional way but in a spontaneously creative fashion that changes with each observance. There are many groups of this type that are involved in the observance of the full moons, the solstices, and the equinoxes.

The aim of all of these practices is the inclusion of spirit in the relationship. *If we think of relationship as a journey of two souls, then these are some of the rituals or spiritual practices that are designed to invite holy energies to join in the relationship, to sanctify it, to guard it, and to guide it along the appropriate path.* As we have said, these rituals vary greatly from person to person.

It is difficult for us to imagine our own relationship without experiencing it in the context of its spiritual underpinnings. We always know in the good times and the bad times that there is a divine guidance that underlies our connection. We lose it with great regularity, but we find it with the same regularity. Each partnership must seek its own kinds of rituals and observances to sanctify the relationship.

Some of the rituals that can be particularly helpful are very simple ones and may even appear to have little spiritual content. In the more spiritual vein, we have learned to pray out loud together. It was a little embarrassing at first, because personal prayer, as contrasted with the recitation of somebody else's prayers, is usually a relatively private practice. But once we became accustomed to doing it, we found that it was a very natural way to proceed. It is particularly comforting at those times when we have done just about all we can do for a situation and we feel the need to turn matters over to a higher power.

It is strange how embarrassing it is for most people to admit to their love of God. To admit it out loud is even more extreme. We both feel better for the practice. There are times when things are just too much, and to turn things over to a higher power feels very good. When this happens, invariably some shift takes place within us and in the relationship.

People have created certain rituals to mark the passage of the day. For instance, some begin each morning by making the bed together. For them, this represents a way to end the night and begin the new day. It is a way to separate themselves from the dream world and to enter the material world. Many people have specific early morning rituals. For some, it can be making coffee or orange juice and bringing it to a loved one. Others bring in the paper and read it together. Still others may have a specific way of trying to wake up the late sleeper. Mornings, particularly, seem to be a time of ritual observance, whether or not these are actually thought of as rituals by the participants.

We have found it particularly helpful to spend time in the morning going over our dreams together and then taking some separate time for personal writing. This directs our first thoughts of the day inward. It gives us each a chance to say hello to ourselves, to get a feeling for what is happening within, and to set our priorities. We can use this time to think of our current situation in a larger perspective. For many people it is a time for meditation or yoga, and these become very specific spiritual practices. The spiritual process is different for different people and may vary considerably at different times in our lives.

It is important in a relationship to take the time to honor the relationship itself. We think that all relationships need this if the spirit within them is to be kept alive. Spiritual energies need to be able to access the two people in a relationship. We must make room for them, and this means time alone when we are fully open to their presence.

Some couples use their vacations together as a ritual, going each year to a place of spiritual or emotional renewal. This is their way of honoring their relationship. Whether they go to their own summer house or to Hawaii or on a trip to the sacred sites of the ancients, the intent can be the same and the purpose can be equally well served. Each of us has certain places on the planet that feel sacred to us. It is these spaces that feed us and feed the relationship. We believe that finding the time to be in these places and sharing them with one another adds great richness and spiritual depth to a relationship. We have had many remarkable experiences on trips to sacred places around the planet. We take our time and find our own special spot at each of these places, and then we generally spend many hours sitting there.

We feel that, from time to time, a ritual of renewal of relationship is important. A repetition of vows reestablishes the original intent and directly invites spiritual energies to infuse the relationship anew. There are times when you might feel that a new direction needs to be taken and that you must let go of the current form of the relationship. At such times, you may find it helpful to actually remove your wedding rings (or, if you have no rings, each take some other object that has special significance to you), bury them in the ground for three days, and then bring them forth and renew your vows with the request that you receive extra guidance on your path. We have mentioned the process of visualization, the dream process, the "being" state, and learning to access the vulnerable child. Each of these is a way of accessing spiritual energies. As we have said, ritual in relationship and the inclusion of spiritual practices is important but quite personal. We have given some examples from our own experience as well as others', but this is something that needs to be developed individually for each relationship.

Self-Containment and Neediness in Relationship

We are each basically responsible for our own lives and for our own feeling of well-being. It is necessary, in the final analysis, to be the responsible parent to our own inner child. We cannot expect our partners to carry the ultimate responsibility for this child. One of the fantasies that we all share at some very deep level is that the relationship will care for this child and we will all live "happily ever after." That is not the way things work in this life.

In addition to the vulnerable child, there is within each of us a very needy child, one who will cling onto our partner with the panic of a drowning person clinging to a potential rescuer. This very act of clinging makes our partner unable to help us, much as it interferes with the ability of the rescuer to perform his function when the swimmer clutches him frantically around the neck.

When you feel this extreme neediness or panic, you can know that you are in a subpersonality that requires your own attention. You may share this information with your partner, your partner may help you talk with this child, but you are the one who must listen to the child, find out what it needs, why it is afraid, and what can be done to help it so that you can take care of it appropriately.

It is important at some time in your process to differentiate between this very needy child and your vulnerable child. Both can make a relationship more creative and both can effectively destroy a relationship. It depends on whether or not there is an aware ego that can use these energies more consciously.

In relationship, the reaction of your partner will automatically give you information as to which child is operating at any given time. Your partner will usually move in closer when the vulnerable child is present and will behave in a loving fashion. However, when the needy child is present, even if the partner begins by bonding in from the good parent, sooner or later the withdrawn parent will appear and sever all connection.

The lack of self-containment of this needy child makes relating impossible. An aware ego changes this because it knows how to express the needs of the child in a conscious way in order to get what it needs and wants. We each must learn how to express our neediness in relationship with awareness. Otherwise it will sneak out in a million different ways and ensure the development of strong bonding patterns.

When we surrender to the process of relationship, we embark upon a journey into unknown lands. We learn much about ourselves, the way in which we relate to others, and how we might best move forward in our own process. We learn who we are and how to behave responsibly both in terms of our own selves and toward other people. We learn about how to truly be with another human being and how to truly be with our selves. We learn how to care for ourselves and how to nurture and protect our inner child in a more conscious fashion.

Self-containment is a necessary element in this kind of relationship. Knowing about our selves, defining our own limits and boundaries, setting our own priorities, adhering to our individual set of values, recognizing our own contribution to a given situation, and being able to differentiate this from another's are all very important. *We can expect the relationship to enhance our process and to lead us further along in our own evolution of consciousness, but we cannot place this responsibility upon another person. We may help one another, but the person ultimately responsible for our selves is ourself.*

Self-Sufficiency in Relationship

Last, but certainly not least, each of us must be careful not to give up too much in relationship lest we give up just what it was that we needed. It is always difficult to determine when we are giving up too much. Listening to our dreams, becoming aware of our own bonding patterns, and taking responsibility for ourselves all help us to see that we do not give up too much and cause ourselves unnecessary grief.

Marie was extremely trusting. She came from a New Age background and had faith that everything would work out well if only she concentrated all her energies upon success.

Marie moved to a new city to be near her lover, Basil. She found herself a job there, but he soon lost his. He asked, from the needy son, for her financial help. Her nurturing mother could not resist, and Marie soon depleted her financial resources.

When she no longer had any money, Basil, the bounder, left her. He needed another woman who had the funds and the emotional availability to support him from the nurturing mother. Marie's distraught and vulnerable child was badly battered. Unfortunately, to top it all off, she now had some difficulty arranging special care for her vulnerable child because she had spent so much money on Basil that she had none left for herself.

Unlike Marie, some of us are so concerned about not giving up too much that we cannot follow the natural course of the relationship. The balance between these two extremes is important. The best safeguard is to allow input from opposing selves and to process both sides of the question from an aware ego.

Glenda only listened to the fears of her vulnerable child and never really let herself become involved in relationship. Her mother had given up everything for her father and had then been abandoned. Glenda learned her lesson well, but she was so careful to maintain her own "space" that she had very little space or time left over to share with George. She engaged in her own activities almost every night after work. She had a women's group, a class in investment strategies, yoga class, and a subscription to the theater. She also had a number of women friends whom she met for dinner on a regular basis. She was so worried that the relationship might affect her performance on the job, that she often brought work home with her. She literally had not a single night free to spend with her husband.

The relationship suffered from lack of attention. Both Glenda and George felt proud of their sophisticated marital arrangement, but this was an arrangement made by two highly developed protector/controllers; the vulnerable children stayed in hiding. Finally, they realized that neither of them was very happy and they sought counseling.

A middle course was steered carefully by Carrie, a woman who was used to taking care of herself but seriously interested in relationship. When she fell in love, unlike Glenda, she was willing to take a chance and make a major life change for the possibility of a rewarding relationship. She moved to the city where her lover lived.

But, unlike Marie, Carrie did not deplete her resources. She also maintained a fall-back position in case the new relationship did not work. She returned each month to her home town where she maintained her hairdressing clients. In this way, if the relationship did not work out, Carrie had only to move back to her home and resume her life as she had left it.

It is often difficult to determine which course of action is appropriate in relationship. Walking the line between giving too much away and holding too much back requires an aware ego. Having to hold these two opposites is certainly a great way to stretch ourselves and to increase our awareness of both our own internal processes and our external bonding patterns.

We have found that, as a group, women are likely to give up more of themselves than men do. This can be particularly dangerous when a woman completely gives up the resources that will enable her to sustain an independent life. She makes herself particularly vulnerable if she gives up her residence, her savings, her job, and most of her friends.

In marriages, we have seen women surrender complete responsibility for their physical bodies to a husband who is a doctor or complete financial responsibility to a husband who is a good businessman. This automatically bonds them in as a dependent daughter and deprives them of the ability to manage their own affairs in a responsible fashion.

Similarly, we have seen men give over to a wife all responsibility for nurture and the maintenance of a comfortable home. This deprives the man of the capability of living an enjoyable life without a woman to take care of his needs, and makes him fearful that if he is alone and sick he will be totally helpless. Thus, he automatically bonds to his wife as the dependent son.

This does not mean the knowledge or abilities of one's partner should not be appreciated and used. It is great to have a partner with medical or financial expertise or one who knows just how to make life feel cozy and safe. What we do mean, however, is that one should be wary of abdicating total responsibility in any area. *Each partner needs to be in a position to survive without the relationship.* This helps to keep the relationship evenly balanced. If a certain balance is not maintained, the relationship will inevitably settle into a bonding pattern.

It is natural in relationships and friendships that the two people have different strengths and weaknesses. This is one of the wonderful things about relationship. We are able to rest into the strengths of the other person and they are able to rest into our strengths.

Resting into a strength does not mean abdicating responsibility for it. For example, in our relationship Hal rests into Sidra's strength and knowledge in the area of business and money management. If he abdicates all responsibility in this area, then we will fall into the bonding pattern of son to mother in this particular area and this will create problems. What he tries to do is recognize her strength and let that strength help to support him, without abdicating responsibility in this area. He must know what is going on and not abdicate decision making in this area. If he does, he will shift into the needy son, and one day soon he will explode and become a very negative father in relationship to something that Sidra has done.

Along a similar vein, Hal has the primary responsibility for scheduling the workshop and seminar programs. Sidra is very happy to rest into Hal in this matter. However, she remains an active participant in the process and nothing is scheduled without her full involvement. Otherwise, she would become daughter to the father, and eventually her negative mother would take over when something would happen that was not to her liking.

The Dream Process:
Relationship as a Journey of Two Souls

A number of years ago when we were conducting a workshop in Chicago, one of the participants, a Hasidic scholar, told us about the ancient Jewish mystical tradition of a sacred relationship. In this tradition, a primary relationship between a man and woman is much more than a relationship of two people. It consists of the man, the woman, and the holy spirit of the relationship.

We like to view all relationships in this context. The holy spirit of which the scholar spoke would then be related to the spiritual striving, or evolutionary impetus, that exists within all beings. Looking at relationship in this light, *we see each new relationship as a catalyst in our personal evolution of consciousness. It challenges each of us to grow, to expand our awareness of ourselves and of others, to deepen our connection to life and to other human*

*beings, and to evolve until we express in our lives the purest form of
our essential being. As we respond to this challenge, we find ourselves
on a journey into never-before-dreamed-of realms of the psyche and
the spirit.*

We feel that at this time in history, when there is a great
need to deepen our emotional and spiritual connections to
one another and to the planet itself, this individual evolutionary process is sorely needed. It is our hope that this process
will have an impact upon the evolution of humankind as it
moves toward an era in which spirit and meaningfulness are
as important as material well-being.

When we view relationship in this spiritual context, we
see it as the journey of two souls. The relationship seems to
have a life of its own as it helps each of us to move along our
individual paths, bringing to our attention new areas of
unconsciousness that need to be brought into awareness. As
soon as we have mastered one lesson, it presents us with the
next. Very little time passes without movement. We have
noticed that this can be a bit disconcerting, but when we stay
in contact with the excitement of this challenge we see that it
most certainly keeps life interesting. We never quite know
what will happen next in our lives. Over and over again, we
have seen that as our consciousness changes, so does our
future.

Each addition to consciousness, each movement along
one's own evolutionary path brings with it new possibilities
and, of course, new challenges, new choices, and new conflicts. New paths appear that had not existed before.

These new paths may be dramatic, or they can be fairly
subtle. In Fiji, we met a mature couple who had apparently
been leading a stable, predictable life. Their relationship had
been dedicated to growth and self-exploration. They had
surrendered to this relationship, trusting where it would lead
them. Ultimately, they ended up selling everything and
moving to Fiji. They bought a large schooner, sailed across
the world, and set up a new life living on the boat and hiring
it out to tourists for income.

On a less dramatic note, there are the daily subtle changes that come about as the result of this change in consciousness and growth. For instance, Ana, a fairly driven young woman who is very successful in her work, becomes involved with Larry, who is more relaxed about life. Ana's pusher makes Larry uncomfortable, and he tells her so. Ana begins to question the wisdom of operating constantly in this mode. She gradually learns, with Larry's help, to relax and take life a bit easier.

The two changes in consciousness that we have just described resulted in tangible changes in lifestyle. At a deeper level, however, when we think of primary relationship as the journey of two souls, we are looking at an entirely new dimension in our interactions—the spiritual dimension. *This brings us to the sharing of our unconscious processes, literally to the baring of our souls.*

There is much trust needed for this kind of intimacy, because our partner will see things about us that we do not see about ourselves. This can be frightening to those parts of us that have the need to know everything and prefer to keep control of situations. To other selves, it is extremely exciting, because in this kind of sharing with another we have available to us an untapped storehouse of material that is usually inaccessible, material that immediately expands our awareness and greatly enhances our growth.

We feel that the richness that this depth of communication can bring is remarkable. Ongoing sharing at this depth reinforces our contact with our own deepest selves. It keeps reminding us of the underlying patterns that can be perceived in our daily interactions and activities. We find that we are encouraged to look more for meaning in our lives, in the daily dance of the selves. And, as we continue to examine our lives together in this way, we find that we treat them with more reverence. What we do with each day is important; each day is a gift and must be treated as such.

There are a number of ways in which we communicate with one another at this depth. We have already discussed vulnerability and how important it is to be able to share with a friend or partner at this level. This sharing opens up spiritual levels within us, for the child side is one of the central gateways to soul reality. We have also discussed Voice Dialogue and visual imagery as methods for establishing deeper communication with one another. Now we will turn to the dream process, perhaps the richest and most exciting way in which we have found to communicate with one another at great depth.

The Dream Weaver in Relationship

When one surrenders to relationship as a journey of two souls, one finds that there is a Dream Weaver working deep within, sending forth dreams that can be used as guides along the evolutionary path. It is an awesome and yet most supportive idea to realize that there is an intelligence within us that can be available to direct the dream process and that wants us to become more conscious human beings. This Dream Weaver is revered in many societies where the dream is used to provide a direct link to unconscious processes, societies in which the life of the spirit assumes great importance. When the process of relationship is seen as a vehicle for our individual evolution of consciousness, the dreams provide invaluable information, giving access to the great data bank of the unconscious. The dream process, therefore, is an integral part of the relationship process.

Each night, dreams review the activities of the day and give feedback in a most objective fashion. They give information about current psychological processes, pointing out our areas of awareness and giving specific pictures of areas where there is a lack of awareness. The more attention is paid to dreams, the clearer their messages become.

In relationship, the dreams of one partner can be understood rationally by the other. There is also a level at which the dreams of each partner bypass the rational mind and speak directly to the unconscious of the other. At either level, dreams provide an inexhaustible source of information and guidance that can be used in the service of relationship.

One of the most effective ways of surrendering to relationship, and one of the most powerful ways of enhancing it, is to share dreams every morning. We have always shared our dreams in the morning before we begin the day's activities. We recommend it as a daily ritual that will honor the growth process and keep it moving along at its deepest levels.

The Dream Weaver has an interest, or so it seems, in a conscious relationship and often acts to protect it. For instance, if we have become too tied in to our partner, we may dream about having an affair, or we may dream that our partner is having an affair. This is the Dream Weaver's attempt to break the bonding. The dream has performed the same service that an attraction to another person can provide, but it presents us with the information more quickly and with fewer interpersonal entanglements. If the relationship has become too mundane, one of us might dream of being attracted to a spiritual type of person. If we have become too passive, one of us may dream of being married to a passive person and strongly attracted to someone more assertive. Our missing selves usually call out to us first in our dreams.

As we pay attention to our dreams, actions that were taken unconsciously during the day are played back at night. Adrienne had been feeling vulnerable all day. As a result, she had been in her judgmental mother when she was with her husband, George. That night, in her dreams, an unknown woman came over and pointed out to Adrienne that she did not appreciate George and reminded Adrienne of his many contributions to her life. The next morning, she tells George the dream. He feels relief and relaxation, for he had been feeling sad without consciously knowing why. His unconscious had responded to Adrienne's judgmental mother the previous day, and the dream had helped restore the closeness between them.

Sometimes the unconscious gives a very direct picture of what is going on with a partner. A woman dreams on a series of successive nights that her husband is having an affair. She finally confronts him and he admits to the affair. A man dreams that his wife is very busy and no longer available to him. He had not realized that this was happening until he had the dream. The couple were able to begin to work upon an estrangement that neither had known about on a conscious level. When we begin to listen to the Dream Weaver and take our dreams seriously, it is like having access to a giant computer with amazing software that allows us to access all kinds of information we did not have before.

Dreams and Bonding Patterns

Dreams can give an amazingly accurate picture of a current bonding situation. For example, Linda and her husband, Bob, visit Linda's grown daughter for a few days. Mother and daughter, delighted to see one another, enter into an intense bonding pattern.

That night, Linda dreams she is gently floating in the ocean, arms wrapped around her daughter. Linda worries about drifting out to sea, but checks the shoreline and sees that they are not adrift. Feeling secure, she falls asleep in the dream, only to wake up, startled, and discover that she had indeed drifted out to sea. Linda panics and swims to shore, grateful to be alive again.

This dream helps Linda to recognize and break the mother/daughter bonding. The dream showed her that the bonding pattern was not a safe one, that she and her daughter were in danger if Linda remained unconscious (asleep) and they drifted off into further unconsciousness.

Objective Feedback on the Relationship

The Dream Weaver works on a day-to-day basis, providing feedback on our daily activities and giving us the information needed to live our relationships in a more conscious fashion.

It shows us what has been going on underneath when life appears quite ordinary on the surface.

It is often the case that simultaneous dreams will address the same issue for each of us. We personally have frequently found that when we both wake up in the middle of the night for no apparent reason, it is often because the Dream Weaver wants to catch our joint attention. Many times, there has been a set of dreams that, between them, carried a single message for us. We find that this is a particularly constructive and reassuring aspect of the dream process.

Changes in Consciousness as Reflected in Dreams

When people are deeply involved in one another's growth, their dreams often reflect the changes that have occurred in one another's consciousness. Pam dreamt the following dream after she had witnessed a deeply moving Voice Dialogue session during which Rob had come in contact with his vulnerable child for the first time.

> We were in a very old beautiful house. I answered the door and Rob was there, sparkling and new. His hair had soft curls, he had no wrinkles, he was slender and dressed in a long, shining white satin kurta. He came in, delighted to show me the lovely old box he'd found, a little painted box. Inside we found lots of little tarnished silver brooches and pins in the shape of cricket bats, balls, teddy bears, etc. We pinned them all around his hem. Then he and my son got in the car which they had turned around (the motor in the back) so that they could drive it back to front.

The dream shows how deeply touched Pam was by the discoveries that Rob had made and by the changes in his consciousness. The images are specific to his childhood, but they speak to everyone. There is a fresh new quality brought to the relationship by this change in him. Pam is also being alerted by the Dream Weaver. Rob is now able to drive his car in the opposite direction, "back to front," and she may well be in for some surprises.

The Dream Weaver speaks quite directly. It can help bring a relationship to a close when this is the appropriate course for it to take. Lisa had been married to Ed for many years. They lived an intensely bonded relationship in which he was the rescuing doctor father to her hysterical daughter and she, in turn, was the controlling sexual mother to his inadequate son. It was a tumultuous relationship that took many years and much hard work to unbond. At one point, Lisa's dreams pictured the relationship as follows:

> I saw a father putting a see-through clear plastic mask on his daughter's face. She could see out of it but she was choking, couldn't talk, and nobody could hear her. She didn't like the mask, but her father told her that she would get used to it, that this mask was to enable her to breathe and to live. I knew that the mask was feeding her poisoned gas and that it would kill her.

When they were in the final stages of their divorce, both trying to extricate themselves from these characteristic bonding patterns, Lisa felt the pull to return yet again to the marriage. This time, however, she controlled herself and did not contact Ed. The pull was there, nonetheless, and showed itself in the following dream:

> I dreamt that I was calling the house where my husband had lived thirty years ago when we were dating. First I tried the doctor's number (both he and his father are doctors) and then I tried the kids' number. Neither number answered, but I kept on trying and trying first one number and then the other. I tried and I tried. Finally, the operator got on the line. She said, "This number is disconnected. The people you are trying to reach no longer exist.

As her vulnerability surrounding her upcoming divorce became more intense, the pull toward the familiar bonding had re-emerged. In the dream, we see her first trying to bond back into her connection with his rescuing doctor father (phoning the doctor's number) and then trying to bond into the inadequate son (trying to reach the kids' number). Finally there is the intervention of her impersonal voice (the operator), someone who is uninvolved but conveys the facts. The fact was that there was no longer any conscious relationship, just a bonded one.

Breaking Family Bonding Patterns

The Dream Weaver can be the catalyst for changing long-term family bondings, which are particularly difficult. Marishka had been bonded into her actual father as the pleasing daughter. As a result, she subsequently bonded with her boyfriends in similar fashion. One night she dreamt she was in an airport. She was looking for her passport and realized that a pickpocket had been taking other people's identities and putting them in her pocket. She could not find an identity of her own. Marishka used this dream to see how she had accepted other people's ideas of who she was, and she was able to separate further from the familiar pleasing daughter.

A relationship can help to break us out of a family bonding pattern that keeps us moving back and forth in the same track. Jerry and Evan used their relationship in a very creative fashion to break out of their old family bonding patterns. One night Evan dreamt that he went with Jerry to visit his childhood home. He had remembered his home as very beautiful and large. He was especially eager to see the big old tree that had grown in the front yard and had been the pride of the family.

When he arrived with Jerry, Evan saw that the house was quite ordinary and, most surprising of all, that the tree was not very big, not particularly beautiful, and that many of its leaves had fallen to the ground.

Evan realized in the dream that his family had always idealized themselves and denied the existence of any problems. Upon awakening, he felt that this dream represented a real change in his relationship to the "family tree," that he had successfully pulled out of the family system and was now a more objective observer of the realities of his life.

The Dream Weaver Gives Advice

The Dream Weaver sometimes gives excellent advice when one asks a direct question before going to sleep. Sandy, in desperation one night, asked for a dream to explain to her what it was that kept her from feeling peaceful in her relationships. The Dream Weaver gave the following picture of how she should separate herself from the intense responsible mother/victim daughter bonding that she had entered into with Ron, who bonded to her from a needy desperate son/abusive father:

> I dreamt that I should keep a sponge between myself and the man I am with when I sleep with him at night to absorb the negativity that comes from him. In the morning, I could wake up and throw it out and I wouldn't have to take it all in.

Relationship Helps to Recover the Treasure

Ben is in a relationship with a woman whom he loves and toward whom he feels a very deep commitment. He is a man who does not commit easily, so for him this is a very special relationship, and in it he is able to express his needs for one of the first times in his life. He has the following dream:

> I was scuba diving and found a sunken Spanish Galleon filled with treasure. I was diving alone and knew that I must have a partner to help recover the gold and treasure. Upon returning

to the surface I ask Anna to join me. Though she was frightened of diving and didn't like the depths, she agreed to help me bring the treasure to the surface.

Here the Dream Weaver paints such a lovely portrait! The dreamer cannot raise the treasure alone. Ben needs the help of his friend, and he is able to ask for it.

Anna is not used to deep sea diving. She is not used to working with the unconscious and she is afraid of it. Because of her love, she is willing to join with him in his attempt to bring the treasure to the surface. How often it is that relationship challenges us to try things that we would never ordinarily try because of our feelings for another person and our commitment to our own process of consciousness evolution.

Sharing dreams has been important for us personally. The Dream Weaver has proven a trustworthy ally in our struggle for consciousness. We have found that our dreams have helped us when help was most needed. It is as though a divine intelligence was available to each of us, awaiting its moment of awakening. This awakening occurs for any of us when we begin to take the unconscious seriously, when we begin to visualize, to attend to our dreams, to pay attention to our different selves. Once this intelligence is ignited, we have a friend, a divine friend, who is interested in our well-being and who wants nothing more than the evolution of consciousness in each of us.

I Can't Be Truly Me Unless I Have You

The fairy tale version of romantic love teaches that once one finds the right mate, there is a marriage and then the two live happily ever after. Somehow the relationship magically brings out the King or Queen in each of us; therefore, our task in life is to find the correct mate so that we can be truly ourselves. In contrast to this, many of us now have a real fear that we will lose ourselves if we "give in" to a relationship and make the adjustments that are necessary in order for it to work, that the changes demanded of us by relationship are a weakening or a lessening of who we are.

Over the years we have found, both in ourselves and others, that relationship presents us with constant challenges to growth. It is almost as if "I can't truly be me unless I'm with you." *When we do not have ongoing intimate relationships, it is easier for the primary selves to arrange for a life that will suit them perfectly. It is easier to avoid our disowned selves, and, if everything is arranged well, we might even manage to avoid all direct contact with vulnerability.* If we are clever and determined, life can be completely filled with work, learning, and play. Relationships can be pleasant but not important or demanding. We can live a life in which only the primary selves operate and all others remain "safely" disowned.

If, however, you choose the path of relationship as teacher, there is constant movement. *We wish to make it clear that we are not talking about just primary relationship, but about all relationships.* In relationship, nothing stays still and nothing is predictable. Bondings take hold and must be examined. Each unbonding brings with it a deeper understanding of your many selves and an expanded awareness. Each conflict or confrontation will invite you to look in the mirror and to recognize what you see there. More and more must be taken within and integrated as less and less can be projected out onto others. Thus, it is in the daily interactions of relationship that you will have been brought face to face with your selves. You will find out repeatedly, and in a most direct fashion, that you are not what you thought you were. In relationship, there are two "consciousnesses" available to process what is happening to each person individually. This, we feel, pushes each of us to keep moving along our individual evolutionary paths and brings us ever closer to who we truly are.

Epilogue

A New Path

Relationship as Guide

There are many paths to follow as we move along in the development of consciousness. In the past, the primary focus has been on the path of the *individual*, and the popular notion was that if we did our own personal transformational work, our relationships would change by themselves. We have learned, however, through much sweat and perseverance, that although our inner work certainly affects our relationships, it takes a great deal of work *between* people to develop and maintain a conscious relationship.

In this book we have presented the possibility of a very different path toward the development of consciousness, one that is based upon the acceptance of, and commitment to, relationship itself as a valid teacher and guide. In this new framework, one is still very much concerned with one's own personal development, but there is a shift in emphasis. All the work of personal development is still done, but there is an

229

added ingredient, and that is the surrender to the relationship itself.

What does it mean when we surrender to relationship? Does it mean that we must give up our autonomy? Does it mean that we sign a legal document that we will never separate from one another? It means neither of these things. To surrender to relationship means to open ourselves to other human beings and to recognize that out of this opening springs an opportunity for a kind of growth not otherwise available to us. This applies to any form of ongoing relationship, whether it be a friendship, a familial relationship, or a relationship with a primary partner.

When we surrender to relationship, we recognize that eventually there is not a corner of the psyche that will not be opened by this kind of co-exploration with another human being. It is easy to be "strong"; all we have to do is bury our vulnerability and we will be powerful and in control. To learn to live with both strength *and* vulnerability is the real challenge, and it is the basic challenge of personal relationship.

To live fully in the world is to live with as many of our different selves available to us as is humanly possible. This means we must learn to become aware of these selves, experience them, and eventually learn to use them with an aware ego.

The greatest difficulty in this kind of exploration is surrendering to relationship while maintaining some level of personal identity in that all of our selves can still operate in our lives. This conflict is an inevitable consequence of relationship, and one that each of us must struggle with all of our lives. We do not have the answer to this dilemma. What we have offered to you in this book is an approach, a direction, a vision that can help you to work with the conflict in your own relationships.

The more we are living in a relationship identified with bonding patterns, the less of our personal identity is available to us. By contrast, the more of an aware ego we have, the more of our personal identity is available to us, and the more all of our selves are expressed. By allowing our relationships to act as our teachers, we will become increasingly aware of our bonding patterns and consequently will develop more of an aware ego, allowing us to break those patterns and to live more consciously.

It seems as though we must all live two conflicting realities at the same time; the reality of the selves, which (with the exception of the impersonal self and a few others) are very much attached to the outcome of things, and the reality of awareness, which is *not* attached to outcomes. The aware ego must mediate between these two realities and direct the course of our lives as best it can.

Thus, in relationship, the father and mother self in each of us is very much attached to the other person and needs to control the relationship in some way and at some level. Awareness, if it is present, does not need to control the other person and thus is not "attached" to the relationship in the same way. The more awareness, the more objective information is available to the aware ego and the less the attachment.

Whenever there is a rejection of the vulnerable child, we know automatically that the parental self is in charge and that the need to control the relationship will be paramount. We find this in many powerful people, even in those on a spiritual path, who sincerely believe that they are relating from a position of awareness, but who, in fact, are dominated by a strong and observant rational controller who guards the domain of the child, keeping it safely tucked away.

Relationship as a Teacher for the Planet

The remarkable process that we have gone through together, and our efforts to experience and understand the complex system of interactions that has governed our lives, has changed us immeasurably. We have surrendered to the process of primary relationship, to all of its joys and all of its difficulties. Our relationship has been a remarkable teacher for us, and we fervently hope that the kind of clarity that has begun to emerge between us can serve to bring additional light to others.

Ultimately, whatever work we do in our search for consciousness must manifest itself in the way in which we interact with our fellow human beings. So long as we do not understand our disowned selves, we will be surrounded by despised enemies and overvalued friends and will be locked into bonding patterns when we relate to them.

These bonding patterns are particularly dangerous when we think of them as a planetary phenomenon. There have always been tribal groups, nations, and religious, political, and economic systems that have represented one another's disowned selves. This has led to many tragic confrontations. We need only think of the Turks and the Armenians, the Nazis and the Jews (and gypsies, communists, and homosexuals), the Arabs and Israelis, the American settlers and the Native Americans, the blacks and the whites, to start to get a picture of how this operates on a broader scale.

We see neighboring countries carrying one another's disowned selves over the centuries, like France and England, Greece and Turkey, the United States and Mexico. The Crusades pitted the Christians against the non-Christian world. We do not say at all that disowned selves are the whole story, but they seem to be one of the major factors in these conflicts. Certainly when we look at the conflict between the United States and the Soviet Union, with the immense cost of the arms build-up, the mutual projection of disowned selves contributes to the problem in a significant way. The demons in ourselves are always more easily seen in the other person or country.

From a spiritual perspective, to see the divine spark in another human being, and to have that person see the divine spark in ourselves, would lead to a profound planetary healing. This is much easier said than done. We must first become aware of the amazing array of selves that live within us and then discover how they are constantly interacting with these same kinds of selves in other people. Only in this way, as we gradually penetrate the layer of selves that protect our deepest center, can we begin to meet each other at the place of essential being wherein rests the energy of divinity.

Learning to live in conscious relationship with our fellow human beings is a complex and rewarding task. It takes hard work, a great deal of understanding, and a strong sense of commitment to the process itself. On this journey, we learn to use relationship in a new way. As the alchemists of old turned the baser metals into gold, so the new alchemists of personal growth are learning to use the conflicts and pain of personal relationship as teacher, healer, and guide for themselves and for the planet.

Again we return to our basic premise, that the task of healing our planet begins with each of us individually. To change the world we must first learn to change ourselves and the way in which we relate to each other as human beings. Only then can we see the divine spark within each of us.

Sidra Stone, Ph.D and Hal Stone, Ph.D.
THERA, Mendocino County, California 1989

Also by Hal & Sidra Stone

Embracing Our Selves: The Voice Dialogue Manual
Published by Nataraj Publishing/Division of New World Library

Embracing Your Inner Critic
Published by HarperSanFrancisco

Embracing Heaven and Earth, by Hal Stone, Ph.D.
Published by Delos, Inc.

The Shadow King: The Invisible Force That Holds Women Back, by Sidra
Stone, Ph.D. Published by iUniverse.com

Partnering: A New Kind of Relationship, Published by
Nataraj Publishing/Division of New World Library

The Mendocino Audio Cassette Series
Audio Cassettes $10.95

Meeting Your Selves	Meet Your Inner Critic
The Dance of the Selves in Relationship	Meet Your Inner Critic II
Understanding Your Relationships	The Patriarch Within
The Child Within	Children and Marriage
The Voice of Responsibility	Affairs and Attractions
Meet The Pusher	Our Lost Instinctual Heritage

These 12 audio cassettes also available as a packaged set $98.00

The Pleaser	Accessing the Spiritual Dimension
The Rational Mind	Introducing Voice Dialogue
The Psychological Knower	Voice Dialogue Demonstrations

Making Relationships Work for You (two tape set)
Making Your Dreams Work for You (two tape set)
$16.95
The Aware Ego (four tape set)
$36

The Voice Dialogue Series (12 videos and 8 audio cassettes)
Highly Recommended $295

To order any of the books, audio cassettes, or videos above call or Email:

Delos, Inc.
Phone: (707) 937-2424 or Fax: (707) 937-4119
delos@mcn.org
http://www.delos-inc.com

About the Authors

Hal Stone, Ph.D., and Sidra Stone, Ph.D. are the originators of Voice Dialogue, a deceptively simple, yet amazingly effective method for the exploration of consciousness. Their book, *Embracing Our Selves*, which is the definitive Voice Dialogue manual, is currently available in its second edition. *Embracing Each Other* focuses on the "dance of the selves," or the bonding patterns that are the basic energetic configurations of relationship. Their other books include, *Embracing Your Inner Critic*, *We Don't Have to Write a Book*, *Embracing Heaven and Earth* (by Hal Stone), and *The Shadow King* (by Sidra Stone).

Before they began their collaborative efforts, they had both worked for many years as clinical psychologists, consultants, and psychotherapists in a variety of settings. Dr. Hal Stone, who was originally trained as a Jungian analyst, founded and directed the Center for the Healing Arts, the first holistic healing center in Los Angeles. Dr. Sidra Stone was the Executive Director of Hamburger Home, a residential treatment center for adolescent girls.

In the early years of their marriage, Hal and Sidra lived and worked in Los Angeles. Between them, they have five children. Since 1986, they have lived on a farm on the foggy, magical Mendocino coast of northern California. Here, they can watch their garden and enjoy the ever-changing skies, the trees, and the ocean. They write, are available for individual and group consultations at their home, and travel and conduct workshops. Since 1982 they have taught in the United States, England, Europe, Israel, Canada, Mexico, and Australia. Their work has been introduced in Russia, South America, South Africa, and in New Zealand as well.

For further information regarding the work of
Drs. Hal and Sidra Stone,
please write to them at
P. O. Box 604, Albion, CA 95410-0604
or see the website at
http://delos-inc.com